BE'ER HAGOLAH INSTITUTES

IS

changing the future of Soviet Jewry in America

. . .one child at a time.

INTEGRATING SOVIET JEWISH CHILDREN
INTO AMERICAN JEWISH LIFE

BE'ER HAGOLAH stands at the forefront of education for Soviet Jewish children. For over 13 years Be'er Hagolah has been providing the highest quality secular and religious education to new arrivals from the Soviet Union. Be'er Hagolah has grown rapidly as the number of immigrants reaching the shores of America has multiplied. Boys and girls from kindergarten through high school count on Be'er Hagolah - 800 children, with that number growing with each passing day.

Mikhail just arrived from Kiev and is learning to speak English in a special "Absorption Class"

Katya is in the U.S. just three months. When her family arrived from Moscow they enrolled her in Be'er Hagolah's Kindergarten

Children who arrive at Be'er Hagolah's doors do not generally speak English. They have no understanding of what it means to be Jewish. They are in a new country. Their parents are usually first struggling with a new language, and adapting their former education and expectations to the realities of the American marketplace. It is not an easy time in the child's life.

MAKING THE TRANSITION

THAT is where Be'er Hagolah comes in. The school has an "Absorption Program" which utilizes the most advanced computer and language aids to teach children to read, write and speak English in a very short period of time. They also learn the Hebrew alphabet and language so that they may begin exploring their Jewish heritage. They are in a warm and supportive environment where their teachers' involvement and assistance does not end when school lets out.

BE'ER HAGOLAH MEANS
A QUALITY SECULAR EDUCATION...

BE'ER HAGOLAH students follow a fully-accredited course of study leading to a Regents High School Diploma. Specially-skilled teachers use a broad spectrum of computer aids to teach children English as a second language, as well as Hebrew as a third language. Students follow a full curriculum in English, mathematics, science, social studies, computers, music, art, physical education, as well as take electives in bookkeeping, home economics, psychology and French. Additionally, students may earn college credits in advanced biology, advanced chemistry, calculus, computer concepts, and physics.

ADOPT-A-CHILD

... An opportunity
of a lifetime ...

... For you and
the child

...AND A RICH JEWISH EDUCATION

OUR students have the same rigorous yeshiva training as students in American yeshivos, with one major difference. Regardless of the child's age or lack of background, there are classes geared to his or her level. We take nothing for granted: beginning with belief in G-d, and progressing through the development of Jewish life and traditions through the ages, concepts are explained and explored with students. Our students learn Chumash, tefillah, Jewish history, halacha, philosophy, and Shabbos and Yom Tov observance. When students are ready, they move on to Nevi'im, Mishnayos, Gemorrah, and other more advanced subjects.

A crucial element of their Jewish education is the opportunity to be involved and to participate in Shabbos and Yom Tov with their teachers, with their "big brothers" or "big sisters", or with American Jewish families that the school has arranged to host them through on-going Shabbatonim. A child's first Shabbos is always a memorable and meaningful experience. The child's first Rosh HaShanah, or Yom Kippur, or Sukkos, or Chanuka, or Purim or Pesach, or whatever holiday that he spends with an American Jewish family, may be the first he or she ever knows.

INVESTING IN THE FUTURE

TODAY'S marketplace does not always allow even the most prudent investor to realize a return on his or her investment. But, an investment in any one of Be'er Hagolah's students is a "sure thing." Participants in the Adopt-a-child Program will be making a direct investment in the future of that child. As you track your child's progress over the years you will be able to see the affect that your support and encouragement is having.

ADOPT-A-CHILD...AN OPPORTUNITY OF A LIFETIME...FOR YOU AND THE CHILD

נפתלי אילה שלחה הנתן אמרי שפר

ספר זה מוקדש לעילוי נשמת

ר' נפתלי בן נטע יצחק דזשייקאבס ז"ל

שהי' אילה שלחה – לעשות חסדים וטובות כל ימי חייו

הנתן אמרי שפר – שתמיד הי' משמח אלקים ואנשים

בדברי תורה, מאמרי חיזוק ורגשי ידידות

נפטר כ"ג טבת, תשנ"ב

This collection of inspiring stories of the Holocaust
is dedicated to the memory of

R' Naftali Jacobs ז"ל

... a survivor of the concentration camps
... whose gentle spirit proved untouched
by the flames of the Holocaust
... whose life as a husband, father and friend
spoke volumes of his love and active devotion
for Hashem, Gedolim and Klal Yisroel.

ת.נ.צ.ב.ה.

RACHEL POMERANTZ

WINGS ABOVE THE FLAMES

STORIES OF FLIGHT, ESCAPE AND DIVINE PROVIDENCE DURING THE HOLOCAUST

CIS

P·U·B·L·I·S·H·E·R·S

New York · London · Jerusalem

Published and distributed
in the U.S., Canada and overseas by
C.I.S. Publishers and Distributors
180 Park Avenue, Lakewood, New Jersey 08701
(908) 905-3000 Fax: (908) 367-6666

Distributed in Israel by
C.I.S. International (Israel)
Rechov Mishkalov 18
Har Nof, Jerusalem
Tel: 02-518-935

Distributed in the U.K. and Europe by
C.I.S. International (U.K.)
89 Craven Park Road
London N15 6AH, England
Tel: 81-809-3723

Book and cover design: Deenee Cohen
Typography: Nechamie Miller
Cover illustration: Francis McGinley

ISBN 1-56062-114-1 soft cover
Library of Congress Catalog Card Number
92-70690

PRINTED IN THE UNITED STATES OF AMERICA

TABLE OF CONTENTS

The word of the Lord came to me, saying,
Ben Adam, set your face in the direction of the south
and let your words flow southward;
prophesy against the forest of the south.
And say to the forest, Hear the Word of the Lord.
Thus says my Lord G-d,
Behold! I kindle within you a fire
that will consume within you every fresh tree and every
dry tree,
an intense flame that will not be extinguished,
and every face from the south of the north
shall be singed by it.
Thus all flesh shall see that I, the Lord, have kindled it.
It shall not be extinguished.

I said: Ah! My Lord G-d, they say about me,
Is he not an inventor of fables?

So the word of the Lord came to me, saying,
Ben Adam, set your face toward Jerusalem,
and let your words flow to the Sanctuaries
And prophesy against the soil of Israel,
And say to Israel's soil, Thus says the Lord,
Behold! I am against you.
I shall draw My sword from its scabbard
and cut off from among you righteous and wicked alike.

(Ezekiel 21:1-8)

PREFACE

Certain eras in history inevitably attract the writer of historical fiction, eras in which tiny events were able to tip the balance between life and death. The Spanish Inquisition was one such era, and the destruction of Eastern European Jewry, both the physical destruction under the Germans and the spiritual destruction under the Russians, was another. It would be a shame, though, for a writer to indulge in fictional accounts of such periods, when true stories are left unrecorded for want of someone to listen to those who lived through them and to write them down. As long as such stories are still being told by the people who lived them, it seems proper even for artists of fiction to rein in their imaginations and assume a somewhat more passive role.

This book, then, is historical non-fiction about the recent period of appalling destruction. The stories cover the decade from 1938 to 1947, the years 5698 to 5707 on the Jewish calendar. The settings are spread over a geographic range from France in the west to Siberia in the east, and the episodes are intended to represent a wide range of Jewish experience from the period, stories of wandering refugees and ghetto dwellers, persecuted civilians and labor camp inmates. Only the choice of characters is deliberately skewed away from the typical range of survivors. The people who appear in these stories all have a sensitivity to spiritual issues that occasionally lifts them above the natural concerns of the persecuted, above the concerns of how fast to eat the bread ration, where to find a scrap of string to use as a shoelace, how to avoid being punished for some imaginary crime.

All the details are recorded as told by the people who lived through them, without embellishment, and all the stories were read back to these individuals so they could make corrections. However, in order to protect their privacy, many of the characters' names are changed. Others, listed in the notes, preferred to appear under their own names. Place names, dates and events were checked through reference works.

This volume includes two sections of stories, most of which originally appeared in Hebrew under the title, *Mikur Habarzel*. The stories in the first section are about the German persecutions, and those in the second are about the Russian repression. It also contains a third section that did not appear previously, a historical account of the period from a Jewish point of view. It is set within a context of two hundred and fifty years, the years marking the events starting from the beginning of the Enlightenment in 1740 to the date of writing in 1990. Most of the information is drawn from the five standard texts listed at the beginning of the bibliography. Direct quotations and other sources used are footnoted. It is hoped that the historical background will make the stories clearer and more significant, while the narratives will make the history more memorable.

I thank all those who aided in the preparation of the book, particularly my husband for his editorial assistance and historical expertise. I also thank Rabbi Yaakov Yosef Reinman of C.I.S. Publishers for encouraging me to undertake the historical essay and Rabbi Tzvi Lampel for his expert editing of the entire manuscript. However, it is particularly necessary to thank those who were willing to relive distressing events and record their stories. Most of all, I thank the Almighty for granting me the honor and privilege of completing this work.

The sagas in this book must be restricted to accounts about the few who survived, for ashes cannot tell a story. We recall the flames of destruction together with the wings of escape. Let the title, *Wings above the Flames*, stand as a memorial to the majority who did not survive.

The German Inferno

Many are the towns in pre-war Europe which could lay claim to once having had a sizable Jewish community. Each community had its own history and customs, its own personality. Like trees in a forest, each one stood by itself, yet underground, each one's roots interlaced with its neighbors', and all the trees' branches, as they reached toward the sky, intertwined with each other. And alas, as they stood together, so did they fall together. The forest fire that swept through the Jewish communities of Eastern Europe destroyed them all in one furious conflagration.

In the first story, we follow the wanderings of one refugee family torn loose from the parent tree by the searing gusts of persecution and sent tumbling through the air like a maple seed on its two frail wings. Most families perished with their home community. But a few, tattered and scorched, fluttered along, always just slightly ahead of the blaze, as wings above the flames.

BLOWN BY THE WIND | 1

T he Polish passport official climbed onto the train when it stopped at Katowice, the last town before the Polish-German border, and went down the aisles checking passports as the train resumed its speeding course toward Germany. Michael Feld, returning home from a vacation with his father's relatives in Poland, presented his Polish passport.

The official asked him a question in Polish.

Fourteen-year-old Michael shrugged to indicate that he did not speak Polish. Born in Germany, he had only inherited Polish citizenship through his late father, but he had never actually been to Poland before this summer.

The man shouted a question at him.

Michael quietly replied in German that he did not speak Polish, but the official continued to rant. Finishing his tirade, he simply closed Michael's passport, put it in his own pocket and, incredibly, marched out of the car.

Michael sat stunned. Here he was, travelling alone through a strange country, with a conspicuously Jewish name, and just as he came to the border of Nazi Germany, he was suddenly left without a passport.

He heard a hiss of steam from the brakes, the train screeched to a halt in the German town of Beutheu, and on climbed a uniformed man with a swastika arm band.

"*Heil Hitler! Deutsche Passportkontrol!*" barked the man.

In a flash of inspiration, Michael realized where his only hope at regaining his papers lay. He leaped toward the officer, clung to him and cried out, "*Heil Hitler!* Save me! *Heil Hitler!* Save me!"

The officer jumped back, startled by the frantic action of the young boy, and demanded an explanation. Michael told the story of the passport official.

"He must still be on the platform, waiting for a train back to Katowice," said the German. "Do you think you would recognize him?"

Michael nodded.

The German left his post and set off with Michael on a search that was entirely outside his line of duty. They found the official quickly, and the German launched into a tirade louder than the one the Pole had directed at Michael. The cowed Pole handed over Michael's passport to his German counterpart, who returned it to Michael. As Michael climbed back aboard his train, he mused over the irony of being saved by a Nazi. Mysterious are the ways of Heaven.

A few weeks later, Michael rapped on the door of Rabbi Dr. Gutmann, one of his teachers in the Jewish high school in Leipzig. Leipzig, being on the eastern side of Germany, had a relatively high concentration of Eastern European Jews. Since, on the whole, the Polish and Hungarian Jews living in Germany were generally more religious than their native-born German brothers, Leipzig supported a vigorous and varied religious life, including one of the few Jewish high schools in all of Germany. Rabbi Gutmann had always been particularly kind to Michael. When he opened the door and found the boy standing on the doorstep, he ushered him in with a warm greeting and gave him a seat.

"I've come to say good-bye," Michael said.

"Where are you going?" asked his surprised teacher.

"To Belgium," answered Michael, "to live with my mother's family."

Michael's goal pleased Rabbi Gutmann. Belgium was politically neutral, allied neither to Germany nor to France. Thunderclouds were gathering over all of Europe, but perhaps little Belgium would escape the impending lightning. The rabbi leaned back in his chair and tried to decide what sort of encouragement to give his student. It is the custom to connect every speech to the Torah portion of the week read in the synagogue. The section for that particular week began, "When you go out to war . . ." How very appropriate!

"Michael," began the rabbi, leaning forward, "you are also going out to battle, a battle for life."

ANTWERP, BELGIUM • 1939-1940

W hen Michael arrived in Belgium, travelling as a dependent on an aunt's passport, he was taken in by his mother's relatives. He discovered that for his getaway from Germany he was indebted to another aunt, the wife of his mother's brother. The clan had gathered one day to discuss the situation of their relatives in Germany. His aunt had spoken up and insisted it was not enough to sympathize, and that they must take some action. She had remained insistent, and finally, the family had taken the necessary steps to obtain a Belgian visa for Michael.

If one woman had not had the strength of character to say the right word at the right time, Michael realized, he would still be back in Leipzig, where the situation of the Jews was worsening steadily. Michael was determined to follow his aunt's example. If a few words could save him, perhaps a few more words could save his widowed mother and his younger brother, who were still in Leipzig.

It turned out, however, that more than a few words were needed. Support and shelter for the visitors had to be guaranteed by the Belgian sponsors of a visa application, and it was easier to obtain such a guarantee for a young boy of fourteen than for an entire family. Michael began going from one relative to another, searching for someone willing to sponsor a visa application for his mother.

The situation of his mother and brother in Germany grew steadily more precarious. October 31 was approaching. It was the deadline set by the Polish government for Polish citizens residing abroad to have their passports stamped or be deprived of their citizenship. To his and his mother's frustration, all her repeated applications to the Polish consulate in Leipzig for a validating stamp had been refused. It was frustrating because they were not aware that the Polish government had no intention of taking back any Jews.

One afternoon shortly before that date, Michael's mother braced herself and returned to Germany's Polish consulate for another attempt to escape the threat of statelessness. This attempt proved fortunate for an unexpected reason, for while she was there, she caught a rumor spreading through the halls that the Gestapo was planning to round up all Polish citizens and deport them to Poland. The dilemma was horrendous. Poland was canceling citizenship of her people in Germany, and

Germany was sending them back to Poland, which was at least as hostile to Jews as was Germany. The prospect of her friends and relatives being sent to Poland, while having their official citizenship canceled, horrified Mrs. Feld.

She raced for a phone and began calling all her friends and relatives with Polish passports, warning them of the danger. She urged them to join her in the consulate, which enjoyed the protection of extraterritoriality normally granted embassies and consulates. She also had someone bring Rudi, her younger son. Polish Jews began streaming into the consulate. It was fortunate that the grounds were spacious, for by evening, several hundred refugees arrived. Unfortunately, however, there were many, many more who did not reach that small island of refuge and instead suffered the storm of violence known as the *Polenaktion*.

The devious Gestapo chose a Friday night for that frightening raid. While religious Polish Jews were sitting peacefully at their Sabbath table, their worries about the future temporarily pushed aside and their pockets empty of money, policemen broke into their homes and hauled them out to waiting vehicles, giving them no time to take anything along. They were to be dumped on the other side of the Polish border with only the clothes they were wearing and not a German mark or Polish zloty in their pockets.

News of the raid spread, even as it was taking place, to all segments of the Jewish population in Leipzig. The owner of one of the banks in town, a Herr Kroch, realized immediately what trouble the deportees would have in Poland without funds. To save them from immediate starvation, he hurriedly phoned the cashier of his bank and ordered him to get the keys and open the safe. Swiftly following the orders of Herr Kroch, the cashier took several bags full of money, hurried down to the train station and distributed money to the victims of the raid as they were being shoved into the railroad cars.

After the strike, the Polish and German governments began negotiating the fate of the deportees interned at Zbaszyn. The Jews who had taken refuge in the consulates, such as the Felds, were allowed to return to their homes, pending a settlement. Two weeks later, they were subjected to the terror of *Kristallnacht*. Mrs. Feld and her son Rudi realized that somehow they had to get out of Germany.

Michael continued his urgent efforts to obtain a Belgian visa for his mother and brother. Eventually, he managed to find a sponsor who would undertake financial support. However, there remained another formidable hurdle in his way. Belgium would not issue an immigrant's visa, but only a visitor's visa, and it required applicants to produce a written guarantee from the German government that if they left Germany they would be allowed to return. This was even more difficult to obtain than the certificate of good character required by America.

Michael sent a detailed letter to his mother, describing the form of return visa she would need. Mrs. Feld set off for the appropriate government office, without overmuch optimism about her chances of success. Entering the building, she explained her request to a clerk and was directed to the office of a senior official in the department. He greeted her with the "*Heil Hitler!*" required by law. Mrs. Feld told him the truth about her desire to join her son in Belgium. The official asked her a few questions to test her story, while making sure to interrupt occasionally with a shout of "*Heil Hitler!*" for the benefit of anyone who might be listening in the next room.

Finally, he asked, "Mrs. Feld, will you give me your word of honor that if I give you this return visa you will never actually use it to return to Germany?"

"Absolutely!" declared Michael's mother, with utmost sincerity.

"Then I will sign it for you—*Heil Hitler!*—but you must not show it to anyone except the Belgian consulate."

Mrs. Feld readily agreed, the visa was signed and stamped and soon she was out of the office. The Belgian visa followed, and she set out for Belgium with Rudi.

Mrs. Feld, Rudi and Michael were safe together in Antwerp, Belgium, but life was difficult. Barely supported by a refugee aid committee and by donations from relatives, they had to rent a very small room with a kitchen. They knew few people, did not speak the language of the country, and their health was poor. Mrs. Feld was suffering from gallstones, and Michael had problems with his legs, the remnants of a childhood bout with polio.

In the late summer of 1939, Michael was sent to a hospital for an operation on his legs. The refugee committee paid for the hospital, and the physician, an eminent orthopedic surgeon, donated his services, operating on the leg in September. He visited the recuperating boy every day, and the nurses assured Michael that he was getting more dedicated care than that received by the doctor's paying clients.

To utilize the time during his hospital stay, Michael began learning French, so that he could understand the Belgians and follow the radio broadcasts. There was a great deal of important news on the radio that summer. In September, while Michael was still in the hospital recovering from the operation, Germany attacked Poland. World War II had begun. The world was in turmoil.

The operation on Michael's legs had partially corrected the difficulty, but it had not been a complete success. One wound became infected, and a new operation was scheduled for May 13. The swollen leg was kept bandaged, and Michael had to hobble with the aid of a cane.

Early in the morning on May 10, 1940, air raid sirens

suddenly began to shriek. Total confusion immediately reigned, and it was almost impossible to gain any solid information from the contradictory radio broadcasts, except that Germany had now attacked the Low Countries, including Belgium, the Felds' "haven." The Germans were claiming smashing victories, and the points at which fighting was reported were progressively deeper within Belgium and the Netherlands. British and French troops moved into Belgium to support the local troops. But by May 13, Queen Wilhelmina of Holland fled to London with her family. The skies were full of airplanes, and refugees were pouring into the city from the direction of the German advance. Michael realized that this was not the time to undergo his operation. Under his direction, the Felds hastily packed their possessions into a few small bundles and notified their relatives that they were attempting to cross over the border to France.

The following morning, they arrived at the train station, where a special train was already waiting to carry refugees south. One of the relatives had come to see them off and pressed two hundred francs on Mrs. Feld. It was a small sum, but since they had no other resources, it was very welcome. On the refugee train there was no fare to pay, but it was very crowded and uncomfortable.

As the train approached the border between Belgium and France, a French Army officer appeared and began to go down the train, checking each compartment in turn. His purpose soon became clear. Whenever he found an able-bodied man of age for military service, he conscripted him on the spot into the hard-pressed French army. When he got to the Feld's compartment, he motioned to Michael, now sixteen years old, to stand up. As Michael heaved himself to his feet, the officer noticed the swollen state of his bandaged leg and waved him back to his seat. The infection in his leg was a continual source of problems to Michael, but this time it probably saved his life.

The train crossed the border into France, and some of the immediate tension relaxed. At Poitiers, the first train station, they purchased a ticket for a regular train, so that they could continue their trip in somewhat more bearable circumstances. They continued riding south, trying to put as many miles as possible between themselves and the German troops. Michael's goal was Bordeaux, where, he knew, there was a Jewish community.

At the station in Lille there was a particularly long wait, and people began leaning out of the windows of their train to discover the cause of the delay. There was another train on a parallel track, and someone leaning out of its window gasped and pointed upwards. Circling overhead were two airplanes, so high up that Michael could not make out the insignia on their wings.

"Germans!" exclaimed a man.

Panic swept through Michael's train, and people started fleeing.

"Don't bother running," called a man from the other train, pointing to several cars attached to it further down. "Those are ammunition cars. If they drop a bomb on this train, it will blow up everything for hundreds of meters around. You could not get away fast enough to do yourself any good."

Those who remained aboard the train stood transfixed by the sight of the slow circles the two planes were making in the sky above them. Were they just reconnaissance planes, or did they carry bombs? If they were bombers, had they identified the ammunition as a military target? Apparently not, for they eventually pulled out of their circles and vanished into the blue sky. Shortly afterwards, the train began to move again. Michael did not fully regain his calm until the ammunition train was totally out of sight.

BORDEAUX, FRANCE • 1940

T he Felds did not actually have much chance to benefit from the Jewish community in Bordeaux. Upon arriving in the city, they applied to the Red Cross for assistance and were sent to La Salle, a small town south of Bordeaux. The relief agency had arranged for the refugees billeted in the town to eat in the hotel's dining room and to sleep on straw pallets in an attached storehouse.

Michael approached Madame Dupin, the owner, to explain that, as Jews, they were restricted in their diet. They could eat the bread and the butter, but not the meat soup. Perhaps if she had some raw vegetables . . . ?

Madame Dupin, a very kind-hearted soul, was scandalized. All three of them were thin and drawn from the rigors of their long journey. They needed meat and potatoes to build up their strength again. Only raw vegetables? *"C'est impossible!"*

Michael was quiet but firm. The Red Cross was trying to find more permanent lodging for the refugees where they would be able to cook eggs and perhaps even fish. In the meantime, Michael promised, his family would eat plenty of bread.

Madame Dupin surrendered, but she continued to search for ways to fatten up the Felds. She made them a steaming pot of rich vegetable soup.

"I assure you," she said, "this pot has never even seen meat. You must eat it. You cannot go on without eating something substantial."

She also made them hard-boiled eggs, and the Felds appreciated the concern behind her efforts as much as the food itself.

The refugees assembled in La Salle were soon dispersed to various small villages in the surrounding region, wherever the Red Cross could locate empty rooms. In the town of Lanot, the Felds were assigned a room with a tiny kitchen and settled in.

The mayor of La Salle, a professor from Strasbourg, travelled from village to village to speak with the refugees and try to help them make ends meet. He persuaded the country people to sell the refugees food at a discount and would not let them charge more than a single franc for a liter of milk.

At one point after the Felds had settled in, Michael took a trip into Bordeaux to find a Jewish calendar and copy down the exact dates of the upcoming holidays and fast days. Other than that, they were cut off from other Jews; most of their fellow refugees were French, with an admixture of other nationalities. Out of a population of forty million in France, several million had been driven from their homes by the German advance, and more refugees poured into southern France with each passing day.

Their main contact with events in the outside world was the radio news in the evening.

On the day Paris was surrendered, Premier Reynaud addressed the French people over the radio, quoting an appeal he had sent to President Roosevelt. Michael went to a neighbor's house to hear the speech.

Premier Reynaud cried out in ringing tones, "I adjure you, Mr. President. I adjure you! You must come to our aid, for we are lost!"

A chill went through Michael. France was collapsing, as Belgium had. His family must move farther southward, immediately. It was already late at night, but he knew that there still would be one more train out of Bordeaux that night heading for Spain, and he decided that they had better get on it, before the borders of Spain were closed to refugees. The only taxi stand in the neighborhood was at Madame Dupin's hotel back in La Salle, and Monsieur Dupin was the driver. Would it be available? He raced for the nearest phone to call the Dupins.

Michael dialed the number of the hotel. The phone rang

once, twice . . . and then was picked up. But instead of the cheerful voice he had been hoping for, he heard the following monotone announcement.

"This is the mayor speaking. I am required formally to warn you not to budge from your place. A curfew has been declared. All travel is forbidden."

Michael's heart sank. Apparently, all calls were being routed through the city hall. And to walk into La Salle by foot to find a taxi would leave no time to catch the train that evening.

There was a long pause at the end of the announcement, but Michael did not hang up. He was waiting to see if there would be any more information given. He heard the mayor's voice again.

"That is what I am required formally to tell you, but informally, I urge you to make every effort to escape, by whatever means you can employ."

There was a click, and Michael found himself connected with Madame Dupin.

"This is Michael Feld speaking," he identified himself. "We would like to catch a train out of Bordeaux to Spain. Is your taxi available?"

"Oh, I am sorry," Madame Dupin replied. "The taxi is here, but only my husband knows how to drive it, and he is very sick. This is terrible. We must think of something."

Michael almost held his breath while Madame Dupin tried to think of someone in town who both knew how to drive and could be pulled out of bed to undertake such an illegal journey late at night.

"Ah, I have it," she announced triumphantly. "There is a man here from Paris who can drive. He is a refugee himself, so he will surely understand your situation and agree to help you. I will call him now to ask him."

Later in the evening, the taxi appeared to pick them up,

driving without lights to avoid being stopped for violating the curfew.

It was an eerie journey, as they sped silently down the dark country roads, not knowing when or where they might suddenly come upon the police. When they finally reached the train station, the driver let them off, then drove off again without asking for payment for his services. Michael was beginning to assemble his own private mental list of the Righteous of the Nations of the World. The mayor, Madame Dupin and the driver from Paris were all inscribed on it.

It was a good thing the taxi had not wasted any time, for they did not have long to wait before the train came into sight. As it pulled into the station, however, Michael began to wonder if all the efforts to arrive might have been in vain. Never in his life had he seen a train so full. People were pressed up against the windows in the compartments, and the platforms at the ends of the cars were also filled with travellers. Michael and Rudi stood on either side of their mother, mounted the bottom step of one of the cars and tried to make room for her on the platform before the conductor could arrive and perhaps tell them that no room was left. The people on the platform, desperately anxious to get out of France before the borders could be closed, recognized that the Felds were in a similar plight, and they squeezed together enough to create space for them to get on.

The train was awash with rumors about the progress of the invasion and likelihood of the refugees being allowed to cross the border into Spain. At one point in the trip, an air raid alarm was sounded, and all the passengers were required to leave the train. When the danger passed, they squeezed aboard again and continued as far south as possible. At the station in Biarritz, on the Atlantic coast, they were all ordered to get off. The borders of Spain had indeed already been closed to refugees.

Mrs. Feld was distraught and exhausted. Michael left her in

Rudi's care in the Biarritz train station, while he went to the Red Cross to ask for a place they could sleep. He was given the address of a girls' school outside of town, which was being prepared to receive refugees. Michael set out first to investigate, before trying to bring his mother. He arrived at the school and located the directress, a slightly plump French Catholic woman, who obviously took Michael's plight very much to heart.

"You must not remain here," she told him. "The Germans are coming closer every day. Have you not heard that the British and Polish troops are being evacuated from the port at St. Jean-de-Lux? They are taking civilians with them. You must go directly there."

Michael pointed out that public transportation was almost at a standstill. The directress was not stymied for long.

"Aha, I know what we must do. There is a count living in the neighborhood who left his baggage with me. His chauffeur is to come soon to pick it up. I will persuade him to take you to the port. Quickly, go get your family. There is no time to lose."

Michael strongly doubted that this chauffeur would want to make such a long detour for three people he did not know. However, the forcefulness of the woman's personality rather overwhelmed him, and he set off dutifully to collect his mother and brother from the train station. The trip out to the school, carrying all their little bundles, was torturous for Mrs. Feld. All three of them arrived completely worn out, and the directress was just setting them down to hot cups of coffee when two honks were heard in the driveway.

"There he is!" she exclaimed, and she rushed out the door. The unsuspecting chauffeur was climbing out of the driver's seat to go bring out the luggage, when this rather portly woman appeared at his side and dramatically gripped his coat.

"Monsieur, these people staying with me. You must come to their aid. They are refugees, refugees from those execrable

Germans. In the name of common humanity, you must help them flee for their lives to St. Jean-de-Lux."

"I can't possibly help them," shrugged the chauffeur. "It is not my car, and I have another task to do."

He twisted his shoulder, trying to shake off her hand, but she would not give up so easily.

"This is an hour of crisis," insisted the directress, raising her voice still higher. "Such petty considerations must be put aside."

"If I do not bring those valises to the count, I will lose my place," said the chauffeur stolidly.

"What are a few valises when human lives are at stake!" exclaimed the woman in exasperation. "I adjure you to help them! Put the baggage on top of the car, put it under the car, put it wherever you like, just make room for these three people right now."

The reluctant chauffeur, defeated by her unbending determination, began tying the baggage onto the roof of the car, while the directress saw to it that the Felds were settled comfortably inside. At last, everything was loaded, and they set off down the hill toward the sea, with the directress looking after them until they were out of sight.

ST. JEAN-DE-LUX, FRANCE • JUNE, 1940

W hen the Felds arrived in St. Jean-de-Lux, they thanked the chauffeur profusely, then rushed toward the port. They arrived just in time to see all the large steamers putting out to sea!

The Felds walked over to a group of refugees standing on the pier, to see if they had indeed missed their last chance. The first man they encountered reassured them, if his news could be called reassuring. True, the Germans were advancing, the French army was faltering, and the British troops had gone out to sea for fear of being trapped in the port. However, evacuations would continue by means of small boats, as at Dunkirk.

Michael looked out at the huge, choppy waves for which the Bay of Biscay is famous. The large ships had already sailed quite far out from shore, and the idea of crossing all that angry water in a frail fishing boat seemed very risky. However, with the German army closing in on them, there seemed to be little choice. Escape in the direction of Italy was impossible, since that country had declared war on France, and Spain was also closed to them.

The Felds would be at the end of the line of soldiers and refugees waiting to embark the boats. The line was just slowly inching forward, and Michael tried to guess how long it would be before their turn would come. Suddenly, word was passed on that evacuations were being discontinued and that the remaining refugees should try to flee to the interior of the land. Michael almost reeled under the disappointment. The ships which would have taken his family to freedom had been in plain sight. Now the smoke of war had obscured their way once again.

But there was no time for bemoaning their fate. Michael moved his family as fast as possible along in the direction of the bus station. Here, at least, they had success. They managed to catch one of the last buses leaving town towards the East.

More than a tenth of the population of France had turned into homeless wanderers, swirled about by the winds of war like autumn leaves. The Felds, too, were blown hither and thither in the area near St. Jean-de-Lux, until one particular gust deposited them in the little town of Hasparren, where a generous woman allowed them and several other refugees to sleep on her floor. They waited there, because they knew of no better place to go. The Germans were advancing down along the Swiss border and along the Atlantic coast as well. Rumor had it that the French were abandoning their treaty of obligations and were suing for a separate armistice with Germany.

News of the armistice and its terms reached the Felds one day as they were sitting in a little restaurant in Hasparren, listening to the radio. When the details of the agreement began to arrive, it suddenly became clear that one little town in southern France could be very different from another. A line dividing the occupied and unoccupied sectors of France was to run down to the Spanish border one hundred kilometers to the east of them, and they were on the wrong side of that line. The nearest unoccupied city would be Pau.

Suddenly, the prime goal of every refugee in the entire region was to reach Pau. Masses of people converged on the taxi stands, on the bus station, on the owners of private cars, waving packets of bank-notes and pleading to be driven to Pau. Every car owner would have been wealthy by nightfall if only he had gasoline to ferry people to Pau. Most car owners did not. The collapsing French army had first priority on the use of gasoline for over a month already, and private supplies had dwindled lower and lower. The refugees went from taxi to taxi, from car to car, always receiving the same answer of, "We have no gasoline."

Michael was among the searchers. Mr. Hollander, a British Jew, had been one of the refugees sitting in the restaurant with the Felds when the news arrived about the armistice lines. He had tapped the floor authoritatively with his foot to get their attention. They must all trust in the Lord. He, Mr. Hollander, would remain in the restaurant saying *Tehillim*, and Michael was to go find them transportation to Pau.

After two hours of searching, it was a very discouraged Michael who returned with his report that there was no gasoline anywhere in town. He was sure that there was no hope of flight.

Anything which could be tried had already been tried by one of the other hundreds of refugees with the same purpose in mind.

Mr. Hollander stood up furiously. "How can you say there is no hope! There is always hope! Have you no trust in G-d? Somewhere out there is our transport to Pau, and you must go find it!"

Michael fled, and Mr. Hollander seated himself again and continued saying *Tehillim*. The truth is that Michael was only running away from Mr. Hollander's angry words; he reasoned that as long as he was walking the streets anyway, he might as well continue the fruitless search for a ride to Pau. This time, he turned his steps away from the refugee-flooded center of town and began wandering through the outskirts.

He was told of a van for a flour company which had gasoline and was ferrying refugees to Pau, at a cost of three thousand francs a head. The waiting line to get on, however, was already three days long. Michael could not imagine that it would take the Germans three days to deploy troops in the area of Hasparren.

Drifting out almost to the edge of town, he came upon a taxi stand of which he had known nothing. The taxi was parked at the stand, and the only person in sight was a man standing by the open hood, tinkering with the motor.

"Excuse me," asked Michael politely. "Is this a taxi?"

"Yes, it is," answered the man without looking up from his work.

"Do you by any chance have gasoline?" asked Michael diffidently.

"Certainly," said the man. "How can you have a taxi without gasoline?"

This was all too good to be true. There must be some reason why hundreds of people were not lined up waiting for a ride.

"Could you drive us somewhere?"

"Right now I'm fixing this motor, but when I'm done, fine."

"We need to take a long journey. All the way to Pau."

"I have gasoline for that," the man said.

"How much would it cost?"

"Let's see," considered the man. "Two francs per kilometer. Around a hundred kilometers to Pau, and then back. We'll make it even. Four hundred francs."

"Apiece?" asked Michael.

"No, four hundred francs for the taxi. How many of you are there?"

"Seven."

"Perfect," said the driver. "That's just how many fit in. Come at one o'clock, and I'll take you."

"Shall I pay you the money now?" Michael asked.

"Who ever heard of paying in advance for a taxi ride? When we get there you'll pay."

"But I want you to take us, not someone else," insisted Michael.

The driver looked up from his work, straight into Michael's face.

"I see you. You see me. I tell you that I will take you. Come back at one o'clock, and in the meantime let me get on with my work."

Michael, his heart singing with thanks for the miracle which had provided this taxi, rushed back to the restaurant with the tidings. But as soon as he finished telling the whole amazing story, his spirits suddenly plummeted again. He suddenly remembered that his family had only a few francs left. They could not pay their share of the four hundred franc fare.

Mr. Hollander, not noticing Michael's change of expression, smiled expansively and said, "See, I told you that G-d would help. I'll tell you what. Since you ran around and got us the taxi, I will pay for your family."

Michael was hard-pressed to keep up with these sudden

shifts in their fortunes. This was a miracle within a miracle. His spirits obligingly bounded back up again.

They sat on blankets on the floor of the restaurant saying *Tehillim*, but the waiting was very hard. Without mentioning it to each other, they all had one ear cocked for the rumble of troop carriers or some other indication of approaching German soldiers. At eleven-thirty, they gave up the attempt to be calm and went to check on their taxi, all seven together.

When the driver saw them approaching, he immediately chased them all away.

"I told you not to come before one. Go away and don't bother me, if you want to travel at all."

Chastened and more nervous than ever, they returned to their post and resumed their wait. Finally, at twelve-thirty, they went out again and stood behind a house some distance from the taxi stand, where they hoped to remain unobserved. Michael gingerly peeked around the corner of the house to see if the driver was still working on the motor. He was spotted immediately, but this time the taxi owner took pity on the little band of refugees and waved for them to come over.

"It's all right," the taxi owner called. "I'm finished. Climb in and we'll go."

No further word was needed, and all seven piled into the car with their meager bundles of possessions. Never had the sound of a starting motor sounded so soothing.

PAU, FRANCE • 1940

W hen the Felds and Mr. Hollander arrived, they saw that Pau was packed with refugees. There was barely room on the sidewalk to spread a blanket and sit down. As usual, the first place they headed for was the Red Cross office, where

Michael presented himself at the desk.

"We are refugees, fleeing from the Germans. We have no place to stay."

Always before, the Red Cross officials had taken their names and sent them along with all the other refugees, who were mostly Frenchmen from the northern departments. This time, however, Michael got a different reaction.

The man behind the desk asked, "French citizens or foreigners?"

The question hung ominously in the air.

"Foreigners," admitted Michael. The refugees who were not French were mostly Jews, Michael thought to himself. This man must know that as well as I.

The official wrote down a street number.

"Stay at this address overnight," the official said. "In the morning, buses will come to distribute you throughout the countryside. There is no room in the city. We have run out of water, and there is danger of a plague."

Was this address a haven or a trap? Cautiously, Michael led his small group there and instantly noticed something strange. Unlike every other temporary shelter which the Red Cross offices of other localities had assigned, this one had guards posted to prevent people from leaving. Still, it did seem impossible to stay in the city, which was fast becoming a disaster area, with its population swollen to three or four times its normal size. They decided to enter the countryside building.

It was hard to judge which was the frying pan and which was the fire. There was no food or water in the building. Families sat huddled on the floor, crying and wringing their hands in despair. During the night, someone discovered a breach in one of the basement's walls, and over the course of the night, most of the people in the building escaped through it, to drift aimlessly in the streets in front of the building. Although there surely were signs that even the Red Cross would not be as compassionate in conquered countries as it was elsewhere, the people were not yet ready to withdraw their trust in it. It was, after all, supposed to be a humanitarian organization.

When they awoke in the morning, they did not even have water with which to wash their hands. It was Friday, and Mr. Hollander was already thinking ahead to the upcoming Sabbath.

"When we get where we are going," he declared, "we will have to get hold of two rolls, for *Kiddush*."

There was no hope, under the circumstances, of obtaining Jewish wine with which to bless the *Shabbos*, but bread is an acceptable substitute when no wine is available.

"Also," said Hollander, "we will have to pray. You have *tefillin* and I don't, so give me yours, and I will pray first, since I am older."

Michael concurred and extracted the small bag containing his *tefillin* from one of the bundles of possessions.

The buses arrived to take the refugees out of Pau. They were attractive buses, and when the people who had escaped from the building during the night saw them, they suddenly began to regret their decision and crowded around the door. The officials were firm. Only people from the building were allowed in, and the doors were slammed shut in the faces of the throng in the street.

But who were actually better off? Those who could get onto the buses, or those who could not? How could one second-guess the possible deviousness of the masters of malicious confusion? The buses threaded their way through the crowded streets to the edge of town, pulled onto the highway and began to pick up speed. Michael tried to orient himself and quickly discovered, to his horror, that they were driving back in the direction his group had come from the previous day, straight toward the armistice line.

Panic swept through the passengers of the bus. Michael found himself dispensing words of reassurance. It was still a number of kilometers to the border, there was no point in losing their heads. It did seem an unlikely direction to take if the authorities were intending to distribute the refugees to various farms, as had been claimed. The frightening conviction grew among the refugees that they were either about to be handed over to the Germans directly, or to be locked up in a camp.

Being interned in a concentration camp had no place at all in Mr. Hollander's plans.

"I can't go into a camp," he said firmly. "When I last saw my sister, we agreed to meet today in South France. I have to be free to search for her and to change my clothes in honor of *Shabbos*."

Michael stared at his companion in amazement.

"There are nine million refugees in South France at the moment!" Michael exclaimed. "How can you hope to locate one person in the space of a day?"

The kilometers had been rolling under the wheels of the bus, and the margin of safety between them and the border was dwindling quickly. As they drew nearer to the demarcation line, the number of refugees walking along the side of the highway increased. When the bus reached the town of Oloron, it slowed to a stop, near one such cluster of homeless wanderers. Suddenly, Mr. Hollander shouted, jerked open the emergency exit of the bus and leaped out onto the pavement. Craning his neck, Michael was able to see his companion break into the crowd and embrace someone.

Michael opened the window as far as possible, put out his head and called, "Mr. Hollander!"

The older man turned around and called out in triumph, "You see, I found her. This is my sister!" Mr. Hollander seemed to be a person for whom miracles came easily.

"My *tefillin*!" shouted Michael.

"Oh, of course." Mr. Hollander pulled the small bundle out of his pocket, ran over toward Michael and just managed to hand the *tefillin* through the window, as the bus began to move forward again.

"Good luck," Mr. Hollander shouted after them. "Remember, G-d will help!"

Instead of continuing on down the highway toward the border, the bus now turned off onto a side road, bumped along for a little way on country lanes and then drove through a gate which suddenly appeared in front of them. The gate was closed again behind them. In front of them were long rows of one-story, corrugated tin barracks, and all around were barbed wire fences.

A group of respectable looking Jews was standing on the other side of a barbed wire fence that separated the courtyard from the barracks. When the newcomers turned to look in their direction, they shouted, "Jews! Don't be afraid! They aren't doing us any harm!"

The new residents were reassured by this greeting and alighted quietly in their new home, the Gurs concentration camp.

GURS, FRANCE • 1940

The first blow fell immediately. Mrs. Feld was separated from her sons and sent to a separate women's division. Lines of worry creased Michael's and Rudi's foreheads as they watched her go. She was terribly weak because of her illness, and the gallstones also made it impossible for her to eat bread. Without the boys on hand to find her something to eat, would she have the strength to do so herself?

The camp was enormous, practically a small city. When the Felds arrived, it held an increasing number of refugees as well as a large number of German civilians who had been interned at the outbreak of the war nine months earlier. One day shortly after their arrival, a brusque order over the loudspeaker made all the internees retire to their barracks. Human curiosity being hard to suppress, many of the refugees managed to watch as a number of vehicles drove in and loaded up the German civilians. The release of the German internees was said to be one of the conditions of the unpublished armistice agreement. The terms of the armistice were too humiliating for the French to want them made public.

One of the many rumors abroad in the camp was that of a refugee camp nearby that did not keep its residents imprisoned behind locked gates. As the full grimness of their situation in Gurs became apparent, Rudi determined to escape and try to locate this other camp. Michael, unwilling to leave his mother with such slim hope of returning to find her, declined to accompany his brother, but did not try to hold him back either. Rudi located a manhole which gave access to the camp's sewage system and vanished into it. Michael kept watch all day for some type of commotion indicating his brother's apprehension, but nothing unusual occurred. Just when enough time passed for Michael to begin hoping that Rudi had really gotten free, a blurred announcement came over the loudspeaker, demanding, "Michael Feld! Rudolph Feld! Assemble all your belongings and report to the entrance gate."

What did that mean? Was there anything besides Rudi's escape which would have singled them out for unusual treatment among the tens of thousands of other refugees in the camp? Michael hurried to the barracks as fast as his bad leg would allow and began packing their meager belongings, consisting of his *tefillin* and *Chumash*, a little clothing, some papers, his diary. When he got to the entrance of their compound, a French officer he had never seen before was waiting impatiently.

"Hurry up," he said. He handed Michael a document and started shooing him toward the main gate of the camp. "That's your certificate of release. Once you're out, hold onto it. It may serve you well some day."

He hurried along toward the gate, somewhat impatient with Michael's halting stride. "Your mother is waiting for you outside," he prodded. "I give you half an hour of safety with the release, but afterward, I can't promise you anything."

The officer permitted a friendly Spanish refugee to help Michael carry the double load of bundles as far as the main gate.

As promised, Michael's mother was outside, her face streaked with tears, her expression fluctuating between joy at being reunited with Michael and distress because his brother was not with him. The French officer gave them no time for discussion but moved them ahead down the road until they were out of sight of the gate. He turned to Mrs. Feld.

"There is no more that I can do for you. I want you to know, though, that I am ashamed for France, for the way she is treating you and others like you." He saluted and left.

Mrs. Feld stood wringing her hands. True, she and Michael were free, but where was her younger son? Up until now, at least they had all been together. Michael wanted to comfort her but did not know how. Just then, he noticed a small figure approaching from across the camp they had just left. On his guard, but not wanting to make any suspiciously sudden moves, Michael waited to see who the stranger was. Suddenly, Michael let out his breath with a laugh of relief. Marvelous are the ways of Providence! It was the missing Rudi himself, walking straight back toward Gurs!

After Rudi rejoined them, they started walking away from the camp. Rudi brought the news that he had indeed found a camp that kept its gates opened and also that its management had agreed to accept the Felds, so the family turned their steps in that direction, with Rudi as their guide. Rudi had been heading back toward Gurs with a somewhat far-fetched plan for getting his mother and brother out. Not, of course, that his plan had been more far-fetched than what actually happened, the full story of which Michael heard only now.

Mrs. Feld had been sitting by the gate of the women's compound, weeping, when a man in a French uniform stopped and asked her why she was crying.

"How could I not cry? I am a widow. All I have in the world are two sons. The Germans failed to take them away from me, but I came to 'beautiful' France, and you took them away from me."

The officer stood in front of her, a distressed look on his face. After a moment of consideration, he said gruffly, "Come with me. Perhaps I can get you a permit to visit your sons. Give me your passport." He led her to the office and stood consulting with the clerk in French, not a word of which Mrs. Feld could understand.

The man took her through the checkpoint at the entrance to the women's compound and left her standing in the main yard while he went to fetch the boys. After a long wait, he returned with Michael in tow and Rudi nowhere in sight. Not until he had led them out to the road and made his parting apology in the name of France did she understand that he had arranged not only a visiting permit but an actual certificate of release. Michael suspected that this officer was one of many with a heavy conscience about the armistice and its effects, men who had not yet learned to bow their neck gracefully under the German yoke. Or perhaps, just perhaps, it had been Elijah the Prophet in disguise.

The other refugee camp, at Audox, did indeed agree to receive them, and this time the family was allowed to remain together. Michael busied himself immediately with the task of obtaining cereal for his mother, since the normal food rations at the camp were unsuitable. She had weakened considerably during her ordeal at Gurs, and both of her sons were worried by her condition. Michael was trying to work out a plan to eventually get medical assistance for her, when a new turn of events spurred him into an abrupt change of action. Three large, attractive buses rolled through the entrance of the camp and parked in front of the offices. Officials unrolled a long list of names and began assembling the designated refugees for "transfer" to some unknown destination.

Michael took one look at those buses, as pretty as the ones which had taken them from Pau to Gurs, and decided that the time had come for his family to get out quickly, before their names came up on any such list. He went back to their quarters, alerted his mother and Rudi, and the three of them quickly put their bundles together, as they had so often in the last two months. They waited until the buses were out of sight, then walked out of the camp and started hiking toward the bus stop. They caught a regular bus to Oloron, the nearest town with a train station.

Though they were able to pay the bus fare, Michael was not sure they had enough money to go even one stop on the train. They had already been virtually penniless when Mr. Hollander rescued them by paying their fare to Pau, and they surely had had no opportunity to earn any money since then. However, if they could manage even a short journey on the train, it would at least take them out of the immediate area of their current danger.

When they arrived at the train station to inquire about the fare, Michael found a large placard affixed to the entrance of the station. It announced boldly that those German civilians who had been interned in Gurs were entitled to one free train ride to wherever in France they wished to go. They needed only to take their certificates of release to the police station, have them stamped by the *gendarme* as authentic and declare their destination. This time, the armistice agreement granting special treatment for German citizens worked to the Felds' advantage.

The French officer had been right when he told Michael to keep the certificates of release safe. The Felds headed directly for the *gendarmerie,* and Michael presented their documents. The police official was satisfied by the certificates of release and stamped them as valid. Unfortunately, however, Rudi did not appear on the release papers. Pointing this out, the official explained that Rudi was therefore not privileged to a free ride.

Michael cast about for something to say. He had no compunctions about lying in a case like this, convinced that they were running for their lives.

"My mother doesn't speak a word of French, only German," Michael declared. "When she was in the office, she must not have known how to explain that she had another son, and that's why the papers are wrong."

The attempt failed. The policeman insisted that he could not authorize a ticket without confirmation that Rudi had actually been released from Gurs. Then Michael had a flash of inspiration. The idea was risky, but remaining in this area seemed riskier still.

"Listen," Michael said. "You see with your own eyes that the boy is no longer in the camp. All you need is confirmation that he was once interned there. If he was once in the camp, the only way he could have gotten out was by being released, right?" This syllogism, though faulty, was accepted by the police.

"But how will we know that he was once interned there?" the policeman asked. Now came the daring part.

"Phone the camp," Michael replied. "I will give you his name and block number, and you can ask them to check their lists to see if they had a prisoner by that name in that block."

The policeman, convinced by Michael's reasonable tone, telephoned the office at the camp at Gurs. Michael waited tensely as the Gurs officials checked their lists. Would there be some note, next to Rudi's name, indicating that he or his brother had in fact left the camp in an unorthodox way? Would the *gendarme* holding the receiver of the phone suddenly get orders to arrest them? Now they were not only guilty of being Jews, they had just tried to impersonate German citizens as well.

A voice was heard at the other end of the wire, the policeman smiled, and Michael started to relax. After a brief exchange, the officer hung up the phone.

"Just as you said, he was in Gurs. Clever of you to think of a phone check, young man. Here, I think the simplest thing, to avoid further complications, would be for me to add your brother's name onto the document." He proceeded to do so, signed the change and stamped it with the official seal of his station. He handed the document to Michael and said with a smile, "Have a pleasant journey."

"Thank you very much," said Michael, with an answering smile. He put away the documents and led his family to the door, outwardly calm, but inwardly tensed for fear there would suddenly be a shrill ring from the phone, with a return call from Gurs. It was just as well for Michael's peace of mind that there were no calls at all until they were out of earshot of that phone and on their way to the train station.

It was Friday already, but Michael did not dare to put off the journey until the end of *Shabbos*. He had chosen Lyons as the destination. It had been conquered by the German troops a few days before the armistice, but it was in the part of France to be left unoccupied, and the German troops had indeed withdrawn. He knew that there was a large Jewish community there and that there would surely be apartments which had been emptied when people had fled from the southern thrust of the German troops.

Their documents were accepted without question at the train station, and they boarded the first train for Lyons. They had to cross nearly the entire width of unoccupied France, from the Southwest to the Northeast, Lyons being only a few hundred kilometers from Swiss Geneva.

After a very uncomfortable night, the Felds arrived in Lyons Saturday morning. As usual when arriving in a new place, Michael applied first to the Red Cross. He was given an address, and the family set out on foot to find it. Upon finally reaching the place, Michael stood for a while, contemplating it carefully. It was a large public building, obviously unsuitable for residency. It reminded him forcefully of the building in Pau from which they had been taken to Gurs. He turned to his mother and brother and shook his head.

"Too much risk," Michael reported. "Let's go look for the Jews, instead."

The telephone book had no listing of a synagogue, but it did have one of a Jewish old age home. Doggedly, they set out on foot again, reached the old age home around noon, from which they were directed to the synagogue. Lyons is a large city, and each new search involved much walking, but at last their goal was in sight. The synagogue was an old building with a large main door, closed at the moment. Michael stepped forward, grasped the door handle and tugged. There was no give at all. The door was locked. The services were over, and everyone had gone home for their *Shabbos* meal.

Michael turned around and looked at his mother, huddled on the steps. Because of her restricted diet, she had had nothing solid to eat for over a day. How could he possibly ask her to climb to her feet again for another possibly fruitless search for shelter?

Michael turned back in frustration toward the locked synagogue. If only he could get his mother inside, Rudi could guard her while Michael tried to obtain food. He began to circle the building and soon found a door with a bell beside it. This was very promising, for it indicated a private dwelling, and someone who could help might be home. Michael rapped on the door, since he could not ring the bell on *Shabbos*. The man who answered was obviously a Jew in his *Shabbos* coat.

Michael blurted out in mixed relief and desperation, "We are Jewish refugees from Germany. My mother is critically ill. Please help us."

The man, startled by this sudden visitation, nodded briskly and followed Michael around the building to the front steps. Together, they helped Mrs. Feld to her feet, led her to the apartment and settled her on the living room couch.

Mr. Eisenman was the caretaker of the synagogue. His wife, distressed by Mrs. Feld's obvious weakness, wanted to bring her a plate of the stew she had prepared for the *Shabbos* meal, but Michael had to stop her.

"She has gallstones," Michael explained. "She can only eat bland cereal."

Mr. Eisenman turned to his wife. "Light the gas and cook some cereal," he ordered.

"But today is *Shabbos*," she protested.

"Light the gas and make the cereal," insisted her husband. "In this case, it will be counted as a *mitzvah*."

Michael sighed. Although saving a life does override the *Shabbos* restrictions, Michael longed for a *Shabbos* when it would be safe enough to observe the restrictions in their entirety.

The steaming cereal was soon prepared. Mrs. Feld was at first able to take only tiny sips of the hot gruel, but gradually she seemed to regain a little of her strength. She finally finished the cereal down to the last bit.

Turning to Mrs. Eisenman, she said, "Thank you so much.

You brought me to life again."

Mrs. Feld lay down for a much-needed nap, and the hosts then busied themselves with providing food for the two hungry boys. At the end of their ragged and tattered *Shabbos*, Michael and Rudi had a few hours of genuine peace.

LYONS, FRANCE • 1942

G etting settled in Lyons when they had first arrived, two years before, had been difficult. The Felds had been supported for a period of time by a local philanthropist named Robert Lehman. They had found an apartment in a building whose previous tenants had fled from the Germans. Michael, who was then sixteen, had gotten a job sewing furs. After he had learned the trade, he opened his own family business in their apartment and was able to save up money for medical treatment for himself and his mother. Things seemed to have settled down, but now, in one night, it would all be wiped out, once again forcing the Felds to go on the run.

The pounding on the heavy iron door began around two o'clock in the morning. Michael woke up, and by listening intently, he could make out muffled voices shouting, "This is the police. Open this door or we will break it down!"

The Gestapo had a branch in Lyons, and it was probably the authority behind this surprise police raid. Pulling on his shoes, Michael ran downstairs.

The building in which they had been living was from an earlier era. All the apartments opened onto a central courtyard, and there was a thick iron door which sealed off access from the outside during the night.

When Michael emerged into the cool night air of the courtyard, he saw the terrified tenants, mostly Jewish refugees as himself, coming out of their respective entryways. Some were in their bathrobes, and others were as hastily dressed as he. The pounding and shouting from the other side of the door grew more ferocious. One of the men put his hand on the latch and asked the others, "Shall I open it?"

"No, no," insisted Michael, running forward. "Don't open the door."

Although he was only eighteen, there was enough of a ring of authority in his voice to make his neighbor drop his hand and the other tenants step back.

"This door was built to take this sort of pounding," Michael explained. "They won't break it so quickly."

"What should we do?" asked one lady, clutching the two edges of her robe together at the neck.

"Go get dressed as fast as you can and throw some things into a bag. I'll stand watch here, and if they get discouraged, we may be able to escape." Nodding agreement, the others dispersed to their apartments.

The pounding continued for a little bit, then there was a muffled sound of voices, followed by complete silence. Was it a trick to lure them out?

The other tenants were beginning to straggle back down to the yard, looking somewhat more presentable, with bundles clutched in their hands. Michael made a cautionary movement, warning them to remain silent. He pressed his ear against the thick iron of the door. Someone had once told him that a soldier on watch never stands perfectly still and always makes some movements which can be heard. Strain though he did, he could not make out any sounds at all from the other side of the door, and gradually, he became convinced that there actually was no one there.

Michael straightened up and surveyed the group assembled in the courtyard. Everyone seemed to have returned.

"They have gone away," he said. "And they don't seem to have left a guard. I'll unlock the door, and everyone must run for his life."

"Is everyone here?" asked someone.

They made a quick roll call and discovered that the Eidelheit family was missing.

"They must have slept through the pounding," said Michael's brother, Rudi. "You go ahead and make the break, while I go back for them."

Without waiting for an answer, he raced back toward the stairs to the Eidelheits' apartment.

"Turn right when you come out," called Michael, hoping Rudi heard him. They unbolted the door, slid it open with a heave and scattered through the opening in all directions. Michael and his mother took shelter in a nearby alleyway from which they could watch for Rudi. Soon, he came through the door of the building and joined them.

"What do we do now?" asked Rudi.

"Take cover as fast as we can," returned Michael. "The police are probably routing some grumbling locksmith out of bed. When they come back to find the doors open they are going to be doubly furious."

They walked through a maze of alleyways and back streets, until they came to the apartment of a friendly French family in the neighborhood, who gave them permission to sleep on their floor overnight.

Michael was certain that if the police had started making surprise raids to arrest Jews, the Felds would no longer be safe using their passports as identification. It seemed wise to leave the city and take refuge in the countryside, where the police were not likely to come.

After several days of hiding in various places, the Felds finally found a more permanent refuge in a villa near Lyons. The owner of the estate did not live on the premises; it was the caretaker and his wife, hospitable French country people, who took them in. They had an only son, but there seemed to have been some unpleasantness between him and his parents, and he had left home. The parents did not like to talk about the matter.

After the Felds had been hiding out in the villa for several days, the caretaker's son Jacques was reconciled with his family and came home for a visit. He helped his parents here and there on the estate. One day, as he and Michael were chatting, Michael bemoaned the loss of most of his family's possessions, left behind in the apartment in Lyons.

"Why don't you take my identity card and go into Lyons to see if anything is left?" suggested Jacques, who was about Michael's age.

"That's a very kind offer," marveled Michael.

He paused for thought. There might be more to be gained from this than a single trip to Lyons.

"If you are willing to let me use your documents, perhaps you could loan me your baptismal certificate, so that I could get an identity card in your name with my picture on it?"

"Gladly," agreed Jacques. "But I haven't a copy. We can go down to the village and get the priest to make one out."

The two young men set out on their errand the very next day. It was a long walk in the August sun, and on the way they entered a tavern, where Michael bought them both cold drinks to relieve the heat. They found the priest at home, and he made out a baptismal certificate for Jacques. Since they had a long way before them, they stopped at another tavern for a cold drink, and again Michael was going to pay, when Jacques held up his hand.

"No, this time it's on me," Jacques said.

"But we are going on my business," said Michael.

"Fair is fair," insisted Jacques. "Last time you paid, this time it's my turn."

Michael gave in out of politeness, marveling again at the other's generosity, which was far beyond expectation.

Immediately afterwards, Michael set out by train for a resort town where, he had once heard, the official in charge of granting identity cards was a very pleasant old gentleman. He registered at a hotel and spent a day behaving like a *bona fide* vacationer, before he applied to City Hall. Presenting the baptismal certificate and some passport pictures, he explained that he had been vacationing in town and had unfortunately lost his identity card. The story went over quite smoothly, and the gentleman in charge began filling in the entries on a blank card he took out of his desk.

"Monsieur Chervin, eh?" the official smiled, contemplating the literal meaning of the French name. "'Wine' is indeed 'expensive' these days, no?"

He affixed the pictures, Michael signed his new name with a flourish in the appropriate space, the official city seal was stamped at the bottom of the picture, and Michael walked out of the building as Jacques Chervin, a Catholic Frenchman.

Rosh Hashanah was fast approaching, and on the way back to the hotel in the villa, Michael bought a jar of honey to be eaten on the festival as a symbol for a sweet year. That sort of luxury item was unavailable in the Lyons area. Going to his room, he repacked his bags, settled his bill at the hotel and set off for the train station.

Now that Michael had usable identification, the Felds said good-bye to the Chervins and moved back to Lyons. Michael found that the Jewish community there had gone underground. The synagogue was locked, and services were held in a private apartment. Michael found the apartment and joined the men in prayer. As he stood in his *tallis*, he was uncomfortably aware that if there would be a raid during the services, his Catholic identity would not protect him. Here, in this comportment, it would be all too obvious that his card was a forgery.

The first day of the festival fell out on a Saturday, and the Felds ate at a restaurant full of refugees, all afraid to speak to each other in public. In the middle of the meal, the proprietor called Michael aside and asked him if he had any alcohol.

Michael hesitated. Except for emergency situations, he would not be able to bring the bottle through the streets, since carrying outdoors is not permitted on *Shabbos*.

"It's back in my room," Michael said.

"Could you go and get it?" requested the proprietor. "It's an emergency."

"What kind of emergency?"

"You see that couple sharing your table? Their baby daughter has developed a dangerous ear infection, and the doctor has decided to operate immediately, but he has no alcohol to use as a disinfectant."

Did Jewish law classify this as an emergency requiring cancellation of normal restrictions? As so often in these cases, Michael wished he had a rabbi to consult. An ear infection in a baby sounded like a serious health problem, and if it required an immediate operation, he supposed the baby's life must indeed be in some danger.

"I'll go get it now," Michael consented.

A day later, the father of the baby sought Michael out to thank him. The child was recovering well. The parents were also refugees, having fled from Holland when the Felds left Belgium.

"You are from Sheveningen?" asked Michael. "My father has cousins there."

"Which family?" asked the man.

A little more investigation produced the pleasantly surprising fact that Michael and his acquaintance were actually second cousins who, ironically, had coincidentally sat down in the restaurant at the same table. The relationship well established, Michael and his cousin, Mr. Silberstein, consulted on the best way to save their families. Mr. Silberstein favored an attempt to cross the Swiss border.

"What do we know about crossing borders?" objected Michael. "The first patrol to come along would probably arrest us."

"It doesn't have to be done blindly," insisted his companion. "There's another restaurant nearby frequented by Dutch refugees, and one of my contacts there knows a man who makes it his business to smuggle people across the border to Geneva."

"Then it's worth consideration, if this smuggler can really be trusted. I'll talk it over with my mother."

Thus it was, through a chance encounter with a cousin, that Michael got the address of a border runner and began making plans for an escape from France.

For *Yom Kippur*, the congregation secretly rented a room in which to hold services. The atmosphere during the entire day-long service was tense, because of the awesomeness of the day, because of the fear of discovery and because of the special dangers awaiting them and their fellow Jews in the year to come.

On the evening of *Yom Kippur*, after *Kol Nidrei*, the rabbi called the congregation to attention.

"It is the custom at this time for the rabbi to speak about the special commandments pertaining to *Yom Kippur*. I wish to emphasize one commandment in particular, the obligation to flee for our lives from the trap enfolding us. If it is necessary to ride on *Shabbos* while you are fleeing, then you must do so. Under such circumstances, these acts are a sacred duty."

Two days later, Michael set out alone for the Swiss border. It had been decided that he would make the first attempt alone, having the greatest freedom of motion because of his false papers, and thus the best chance of escape in case of treachery.

If he found that the border runner got him across as promised, he would telegram his family and friends in code, so that they could follow the same route.

He found the smuggler at the address he had been given, and they made their arrangement. He paid the fee, which was not exorbitant, considering the risk involved. It was the season of the full moon, but the weather reports indicated that the following night, Friday, would be clouded and rainy, which would facilitate undetected escape. The man therefore scheduled the attempt for midnight. He gave Michael the address of an inn near the border whose proprietress was in his confidence.

Most of the guests had rooms upstairs, but Michael was assigned a chamber on the ground floor. Excitement kept him from getting much rest. At midnight, he heard the awaited tap on the window, and he opened it to admit his guide. The man wanted to rest and warm up a little before setting out, so it was not until nearly one o'clock that the two set off through the neighboring fields. Michael had three Swiss francs which the woman managing the inn had given him to pay the trolley fare into Geneva, and the smuggler gave him a bundle of maps to aid him once he was on Swiss soil.

It was drizzling lightly. The overcast sky made it difficult to see more than a few yards ahead, but Michael's guide proceeded with perfect confidence along a bewildering sequence of paths and tracts. The wind rose, and the rain began to fall more heavily as they proceeded.

The smuggler ahead of him held up a warning hand, and Michael realized that the path of thick undergrowth they were following ended a few feet ahead in a clearing. They advanced cautiously, and Michael saw they had come to the edge of an artificially cleared strip of land running as far as he could see left and right. Halfway up the strip stretched a tall barrier built of wooden poles and tangled barbed wire. On the other side of that fence, Michael realized, had to be Switzerland.

They waited in silence for a long time, to see if any guards were patrolling the line. There was no motion at all anywhere in sight. Apparently, the heavy rain that was pouring down on their caps and trickling into the collars of their coats also succeeded in discouraging the guards from venturing out of their guard posts. At a signal from the guide, Michael began crawling after him across the open ground toward the fence. The smuggler gathered together the strands of barbed wire and held them up high enough for Michael to squeeze under on his stomach, getting himself completely smeared with mud in the process. The two men separated and crawled for cover, each on a different side of the border. When he was safely hidden by the undergrowth on the other side of the cleared strip, Michael climbed to his feet.

With the first step he took on Swiss soil, Michael felt a tremendous surge of joy well up in his heart. He knew that the danger was far from over, for there had been many cases of refugees being sent back. That worry, though, was like a fragile cobweb when compared to the glorious fact that he was walking on free land.

There was no letup in the rain. Every inch of Michael's body was soaked many times over, and his shoes sloshed with water from wading across rain-filled ditches. Smugglers' routes are never paved. Michael was exhausted, starving and cold, but none of that discomfort had the power to quench that new flame of joy. He had grown up under the shadow of a beast of prey, and for over two years he had been running and hiding. How many times had the Holy Blessed One snatched him out from between the jaws of the beast! Now, for the first time since he was a youngster of fourteen years, he was out of its shadow and into the light.

GENEVA, SWITZERLAND • 1942

M ichael's spiritual yearnings did not skip a beat after his physical salvation. As soon as he reached the outskirts of Geneva, he inquired after the synagogue and turned his steps thither. Where else would he rather be on a day which was both *Shabbos* and the first day of the festival of *Sukkos*? But Michael's mud-bespattered garments stood out in stark contrast to the holiday garb of the other congregants, and when Michael wanted to enter and take a prayer book, they prevented him from doing so.

"I'm sorry to disappoint you," apologized one of the officers of the synagogue. "But I'm afraid we cannot allow you to pray."

Not pray? How can you stop a Jew from praying?

"What do you mean?" asked a puzzled Michael.

"We have orders from the police that all refugees must proceed immediately to the police station to register, without stopping first to pray with the congregation."

Michael was disappointed, but the joy welling in his heart carried him through this setback in good spirits. Indeed, this was not a time to pray, even the *Sukkos* service. If the rain held, perhaps another escapee could come through soon; in any event, the family had to know at once that the route was a good one and that the smuggler could be trusted. All he needed was some money to send a telegram.

"Before I report to the police," said Michael, "I must send a telegram. It is a matter of life and death."

"Go at once to the office room," said the officer. "There are people waiting there day and night to receive refugees and provide them with money. They will give you funds for the telegram."

No one in the synagogue, of course, was carrying any money, since it was a holy day.

Michael turned to leave the room when a voice was heard from the women's balcony.

"Wait! Tell him to wait a moment."

Michael obligingly waited in the entrance hall until the lady who had called emerged from the women's section and preceded Michael outside. Tucking her chin into her coat for protection against the gusts of rain, she called, "Follow me!" to Michael and led him across the street to a Gentile coffee shop. She pushed open the door of the shop, letting in a blast of cold wind, and the sodden Michael followed at her heels. Searching out the proprietor, the lady indicated her bedraggled companion and requested a cup of hot coffee, promising payment the following week.

The owner, who had maintained his store across from the synagogue for many years, seemed to have had some inkling of the problem of Sabbath and holiday payments, for he acquiesced readily. His benefactress, waiting until Michael was seated with a steaming cup of coffee in front of him, wished him a good *Shabbos* and a good *Yom Tov*, and vanished through the door.

Michael had known that he was cold, but he had not realized how tired he was until he sat down. Each sip of hot coffee sent waves of warm energy through his limbs. He stood up with renewed strength for the tasks before him. Until this moment, his movement had been fueled by joy alone. Now that excitement was bolstered by caffeine. It was a prosaic addition, but a necessary one.

The offices of the congregation were open, as promised. Michael accepted only enough money to cover the cost of the telegram, not wanting to carry coins on *Shabbos* unnecessarily. The post office was not hard to find. As he dictated the message, he felt that with each word of the text, he was accelerating the rescue of his family and friends. The joy at his own release returned with redoubled strength.

The buoyant feeling did not begin to ebb away until the telegram had been sent, and Michael was out in the drizzling rain again, slogging towards the police station to register as a refugee. Now that the message had been sent and there was nothing more he could do to aid his family, he began to feel physically depleted, like a balloon with a slow leak. Each step required a greater effort of will. He began to remember how long it had been since he had last slept, eaten or rested.

When his exhaustion reached such proportions that he was staggering slightly, he leaned against a lamp post to take stock of the situation. Just a few steps away was an automat, the door open, looking bright, warm and inviting. In his pocket was one Swiss franc, change from the telegram. Should he have another cup of coffee?

Michael felt himself in a quandary. It was one thing to accept a cup of coffee as a present, as he did before, but it was another thing altogether to pay money for one on *Shabbos*. On the other hand, perhaps without this coffee, he would collapse completely. His head seemed stuffed with cotton, making it hard to judge the situation, and the insistent voice of hunger kept prodding him. He wanted that cup of coffee terribly.

On *Yom Kippur*, the rabbi had emphasized that they were permitted to do everything necessary to be saved. He was still a refugee, still in danger of being sent back across the border. He was not certain that the rabbi's words still applied to him, but he decided to rely on them. He turned his unsteady steps toward the automat, slipped the coin into the proper slot and sank down gratefully into a waiting chair, with the coffee cup warming his hands and the coffee warming his chest.

If he had known that that cup of coffee would weigh on his conscience for at least forty years thereafter, perhaps he would have preferred to crawl to the police station. To this day, he is not sure whether he made the right choice.

When the last drop of coffee was gone from the cup, Michael stood up and set off for the police station again with a much steadier step. He dutifully filled out and signed all the forms that the police presented to him. He was driven to a refugee camp, given a meal and assigned a bed. Removing the wettest of his outer garments, he wrapped himself in a blanket, laid his head on his pillow and fell asleep.

When Michael awoke, his resolve not to postpone praying on *Sukkos* was still strong. One fellow Jew in the camp, Mr. Samuel Keil, had a prayer book and began collecting ten of the refugees to form a quorum for the afternoon service. Due to the shortage of prayer books, they could not each read at his own pace from his own book, as was the usual European custom. Instead, Mr. Keil read aloud, and the others repeated the words one by one. The style was awkward, but the inner substance of the prayers rang through clearly. The men were gathered together to praise their Creator, Who had given them life and spared them from death. Together they recited, "May His great Name be blessed forever and ever!"

MARGES, SWITZERLAND • 1942

Michael's telegram had the desired effect. Mrs. Feld and Rudi succeeded in crossing the border safely through the same contacts that Michael himself had used. Nevertheless, the following months were difficult for Michael. His leg became infected again, and he had to spend several months in medical treatment in Geneva. There, a hospitable local family cared for him as if he were a son.

Once Michael could walk around again, he suffered a different kind of restlessness. For nearly four years, he had carried the responsibilities of the head of the family, had managed their escapes and had arranged their support. Now, he found himself inhibited while being transferred through a succession of refugee camps. Although in each camp the religious Jews organized themselves to arrange for kosher food, prayer services and religious supplies, and Michael found a certain amount of work with which to occupy himself, this was not enough to give him satisfaction. He would have liked to continue, in some form, the education which had been interrupted four years earlier, but there was no suitable schooling available. These thoughts led him to become an activist in providing religious education for the Jewish refugee children. He arranged an interview with the non-Jewish Red Cross woman in charge of rescuing Jewish children from Hitler. She did wonderful work, but she was known as a very difficult person to deal with.

After Michael had presented his request, she said sharply, "I can't provide a Jewish education. I get the children out, I see to it that they have food to eat and clothing to wear, but I can't give them a Jewish education. If you want that, you will have to open your homes to them."

Michael had to admit that she was completely correct. The Rescue Committee, the Vaad Hatzalah, which in Switzerland was organized by the Sternbuch family in Montreux, tried to find some way of taking over the care of the children and giving them a proper education. Since they could not find enough Jewish foster homes willing to take them in, they set up a special camp for refugee children in Marges. Michael was offered, and he accepted the position as a counselor.

He had the normal responsibilities, looking after the children's needs, teaching them, comforting them in their sorrows. However, he had a task outside the camp as well— recruitment. Many children were smuggled across the border without their parents. There was an entire "underground rail-road" bringing both children and adults to Switzerland from Belgium, through France. Frequently, the children were placed with Gentile foster families by the Swiss authorities. Many had been living in such homes for months or years and were often dearly loved by their foster parents. Attempting to transfer them to an institutional setting where they would remain aware of their Jewish heritage was a difficult matter, requiring tact and persuasiveness. Both the authorities and the foster parents had to be convinced that this would be in the best interests of the child.

On one occasion, in an attempt to obtain financial backing for these efforts, Michael requested an interview with Mr. Goldberg, an officer in one of the large Jewish philanthropic organizations. The man would give him an hour, but only on *Shabbos*. Emptying everything out of his pockets, Michael set out on a hike which put considerable strain on his bad leg. Normally, when arriving for such an interview, he would present one of his printed business cards, indicating he was a representative of the Jewish religious refugees' organization. However, this time he had to come without his cards.

He was offered a seat. Mr. Goldberg leaned back in his chair and lit a cigar.

"Since you took the liberty of coming here on *Shabbos*," said Mr. Goldberg, "I feel free to smoke on *Shabbos*."

"Not at all," said Michael. "There was no violation of *Shabbos* in my journey, since I walked here without carrying anything. It's true that I want to speak about money, but since it is for a *mitzvah*, it is permitted."

Mr. Goldberg sat up in his chair and looked at Michael with greater respect. He put down his cigar.

"All right," Mr. Goldberg said. "Tell me about it."

Michael explained the nature and purpose of his school. He

stressed that most of the children he dealt with were originally born into religious families.

"You know what happened to the Jews of Poland," Michael pleaded. "Imagine those parents who were caught in that trap, who succeeded in sending their children out to freedom, thinking they had insured their family some continuity among the Jewish people. Can you stand aside watching that flicker of hope being extinguished because the child is converted by his Gentile foster family?"

Mr. Goldberg swung his chair away from Michael and looked down pensively at the floor.

"My own conscience isn't clear on this subject," Goldberg said. "Someone has been writing to me from America asking me to rescue his brother's children, who are in just such a situation. I haven't known what to do about it, so I haven't answered."

Goldberg rummaged in his desk until he found one of the letters on the subject.

"I will hand the matter over to you," said Goldberg. "Perhaps you will be able to do something about it."

He gave the letter to Michael, who perused it. Every line expressed the writer's aching frustration in hoping to save some remnant of his brother's family, while trapped on the other side of the Atlantic, unable to elicit the necessary action from the Jewish bureaucratic apparatus in Switzerland. The uncle explained that the members of the foster family were apparently devoted Christians, so much so that they even had a private chapel in their home.

"It sounds as though the children may convert at any moment, if they haven't already," said Michael. "I will take the letter and go there today."

"I would really appreciate that very much. As I said, this matter has been weighing on me," said Mr. Goldberg. "But we can't do anything through official channels. Our position is too precarious. As for the other matter, I will try to get your organization a grant of money. Contact me during the week."

Michael proceeded to the address given in the letter. He tried to persuade the foster parents to respect the wishes of the martyred parents regarding the children's religion, and to reassure the foster family that the children would be well treated. He met only a cold refusal. The children had made their decision and would be baptized shortly. Michael was not allowed to see them or speak to them. Defeated, he left. Perhaps, when the war would be over, the family in America would have some legal recourse, but he doubted that there would be any success in recovering the children. This family seemed too wealthy and too powerful.

Not all attempts to rescue children were failures, however, and Michael did regain a sense of well-being in feeling that he was accomplishing something. But this was suddenly interrupted when he was taken with a mysterious respiratory ailment. Congestion, an eye infection, bronchitis—everything together. When he got to the point where he could scarcely breathe, the doctor had him hospitalized. He lay in the bed, struggling for breath, feeling terribly sorry for himself. How much of his life had he spent lying in bed staring at the ceiling? How much more would he spend that way? Here he was, a cripple, unable to breathe. Who would ever be willing to marry him? He worked himself into a severe fit of depression.

Day after day, he lay in bed, contemplating a bleak, lonely future. One of the other counselors came to visit him, and he poured out to her his worries and self-pity.

She began to scold him. "Why are you going on that way? You are a young man, soon you will recover and G-d willing, you will get married and raise a family."

"But it's not just this," Michael retorted. "There is the polio too. What woman will be willing to take me in this condition?"

"Nonsense," she chided him. "Don't be silly. I happen to be engaged, but if I weren't, I wouldn't pay any attention to such things. I would be willing to marry you. And just as I would, so will some other woman. Stop being foolish!"

Michael felt that she meant those words from the depths of her heart, and he believed her. The words broke through the shell he had built around himself. His depression ceased, and he began looking forward to recovery and a brighter future.

Michael's medical problems turned out to be allergic in origin, and they cleared up when the ragweed season passed. He realized his fond dream of returning to Torah study, and for a while attended a *yeshivah* in Montreux. Then, when it became possible, the Felds moved to Israel. Mrs. Feld remarried, and Michael and Rudi both opened successful businesses.

Today, with eleven sons and sons-in-law enrolled at various *kollelim* in Bnei Brak, Michael looks forward to a day when a yet larger third generation will enter the doors of the *yeshivos*. Michael devotes his evenings to philanthropy, and in fact is the mainstay of one entire *yeshivah*.

One of Michael's favorite quotes is from the Ramban's commentary on *Exodus* (13:17), saying the events in our lives are "all miracles; there is nothing natural in them." That a large tree can grow from a tiny seed, that one body can act on another without touching it, that we can see what is in front of us—these are all marvelous occurrences, but our sense of wonder has been dulled by their constant repetition. When open miracles were done for Michael, it made him more aware of all the miracles of his daily life. With his awakened sense of wonder, he looked back over the events of his life and saw Divine supervision behind many other small events which at the time had seemed perfectly natural. How much deeper his gratitude for his escape, when he saw how carefully it was prepared!

Not all of us are saved from an inferno by open miracles. If we were, perhaps we would share Michael's sense of gratitude. But need we wait for such dangers and such salvation? As another survivor expressed it, how much more gratitude is owed by one who never had to suffer those dangers at all!

Even the greatest of forest fires do not reach their full fury in an instant. In Poland, where the lightning German conquest of 1939 set afire the verdant forest of Jewish communities, the process was particularly protracted. The smaller trees would go first, entirely consumed by the flames. Then the fire would attack the forest giants, licking up from underneath. Branch after branch would burn through and fall to the ground. Ultimately, the trunk itself would topple and crash, scattering sparks in all directions. Only blackened stumps would remain.

Encircled entirely by the flames, the Polish Jews had little chance to escape. The few who survived had to endure the inferno for six long years.

SURROUNDED | 2

S hmuel Rubin was a tender eleven-year-old when the bombs began to fall on the airfield near his family's home in Krosno, Galicia. It was Friday, September 1, 1939, the first day of the war.

Shmuel's father had a sister in his hometown, Korczyna, which was just a few kilometers away. The family moved in with her after swiftly packing up whatever they could. But they immediately learned that her husband had already fled eastward. The ruthless Germans were advancing swiftly, and it was said that as they conquered towns, they took away the men, and there was no word of their return. Mr. Rubin therefore decided to take Shmuel and flee with him to Dinov, which he hoped would be more secure, while Mrs. Rubin would stay with the small children in Korczyna.

No one could mistake a *Shabbos* in the *shtetl* of Korczyna for an ordinary weekday. Inhabited almost entirely by Jews,

Sabbath peace would enfold the entire town. The children dressed up, the women decked themselves with pearls, and the head of each household put on his *shtreimel*, the fur hat which was his crown of glory. The townspeople were generally *chassidic*, and Jews from the town would occasionally travel to visit one or another of the *chassidic rebbes* in Galicia.

The peace of *Shabbosim* and holidays was one of the first things destroyed by the German conquerors. The German attack on Poland occurred two weeks before *Rosh Hashanah*, at the end of the Jewish year of 5699.

The roads on the way to Dinov were full of desperate refugees, sometimes groups of men and sometimes entire families. To their relief, Shmuel and his father made it to Dinov without seeing any soldiers, and they found themselves lodgings.

The first day of the *Yom Tov*, the Jews prayed together in the *shul* without being molested. On the second day, Shmuel, standing next to his father, heard the whisper of a rumor passing through the congregation, and then panic broke out.

"The Germans! They've surrounded the *shul*! Everyone flee!"

The terrified crowd surged toward the windows. Shmuel and his father pushed forward with the others and squeezed through the narrow windows, dropping to the ground in the alleyway along the side of the *shul*. They slipped through the back streets, hearing behind them the wild shouts and commotion as the Germans ruthlessly captured those who failed to escape in time.

The rest of the day, Shmuel and his father remained in hiding in their lodgings. On the following day, the Fast of Gedaliah, the German troops began house-to-house searches in the Jewish section. This time there was no way to escape. A German soldier seized Shmuel's father.

THE GERMAN INFERNO • 71

"Another bearded rabbi! Here, hold him for me," he said to his companion, as he pulled out his knife. "Filthy Jew!" he shouted at Mr. Rubin, adding a barrage of curses. "I'll shave that lice nest so close it will never grow back."

He hacked away at Mr. Rubin's face, cutting away chunks of beard together with the skin underneath. Fiendishly satisfied by his wicked cruelty, he left him, bleeding and shocked, and went off with his comrade to the next apartment in search of more Jews to terrorize.

While the soldiers had been in the room, Shmuel could only stand aside, paralyzed with fear. Now he rushed forward and helped his weak and bleeding father onto a pallet. Part of the shock was seeing his father, always such a powerful and decisive figure in Shmuel's world, thrust by the war into a position of such helplessness.

A fellow refugee bandaged Mr. Rubin's wounded face. However, without the necessary medical attention, the wounds soon grew infected, and Mr. Rubin lay weak and feverish for three days. Finally, he had Shmuel gather his small bundle together, and they set out on another dangerous journey through the countryside, back to Korczyna.

When they finally reached home, they discovered that the scourge had hit Korczyna just as hard. On the first day of *Rosh Hashanah*, most Korczyna Jews had formed small prayer quorums in private houses, afraid to assemble publicly. Their fears were well founded, for the Germans did storm into the *beis midrash*, hauling out the few Jews who were there and, knowing that this was a Jewish day of purity, forced them to clean filth.

The first soldiers to be quartered in the *shtetl* were Austrians. In utter disdain for Jewish worship, they stabled their horses inside the *beis midrash* and bragged to their commander about how thoroughly they had desecrated the Jewish prayer house. Anti-Semitic placards appeared on the walls of the town, and the native Poles, seeing how low the Jews were being pushed, joined the game by seizing Jews in the streets and cutting off their *peyos*. After a few months, the Austrian troops withdrew, but the German presence was maintained. The Gestapo office in Krosno now executed its orders through the Polish police and the Judenrat.

In such times, sustaining a family was very difficult, particularly a family of ten. Mr. Rubin never recovered his health, and the task of supporting the family fell upon the older children. Shmuel's sister Bella devised an enterprise to bring some food to the family table. She and Shmuel would buy a bolt of cloth from a fabric factory in town. They then would travel through the farmland, in a radius of several miles around the *shtetl*, and exchange lengths of cloth for potatoes and wheat. This hard, tiring and dangerous work, which involved carrying heavy loads for long distances through a progressively more hostile countryside, brought them grain, which they could take to the mill to be ground into flour, from which their mother would bake bread for the family. However, though this helped them gain sustenance, it did not alleviate Mr. Rubin's torturous situation. After suffering two years of lingering illness, Shmuel's father finally passed away. The tragedy occurred five months after another one that affected the entire *shtetl*.

In June of 1941, German troops were seen again, but this time they did not stop in Korczyna. They walked through the town silently, single file, in small groups of thirty, their helmets covered with branches for camouflage. Strangely, they were marching eastward, apparently in the direction of the previously quiet border with Russia, their ally. Soon, the meaning of this maneuver became clear. Germany turned on her former ally in a surprise attack. The German Empire, like the Babylonian Empire, had to consist of "me and nothing else." (*Isaiah* 47:10) Now, instead of being a back-corner, Galicia was along the supply lines of one of the most massive military campaigns in history.

The *shtetl* Jews did not escape the second wave of persecutions, which came in the wake of the attack on Russia. Their businesses were closed, and it was forbidden for Jews to buy or read a newspaper. And the Germans decreed that the Jews must surrender to the Judenrat all fur and feather objects in their possession, to aid in clothing the million soldiers being maintained in the East. If anyone was found to have retained some moth-eaten fur object he had thought could be of no use to anyone, he was summarily shot on the spot.

A deadline was set for Korczyna, to be followed by house-to-house searches by the Gestapo. The threat of execution had been carried out ruthlessly in Krosno, and the Korczyna Jews, dreading a repetition of that slaughter, turned over everything, including their caps, gloves, coats, muffs, wraps and vests. Saddest of all, the head of each family was forced to turn over his beloved *Shabbos* fur hat. Two days later came the dreaded house-to-house search. The soldiers peered into every hole, into every crack but, to the Jews' fragile relief, found nothing that had been held back.

But the ordeal was far from over. In Krosno lived Inge, a girlfriend of Bella's, and one day soon after the search, Shmuel and Bella went to visit her on their way home from business. After their visit, Inge set out to accompany her friends a short way.

It was cold, and they were bundled up as warmly as they could be without furs. Inge had her hands in a cloth muff, with a tiny decorative strip of fur on the front, too small to give any real warmth. As they walked, they talked about the grim situation in which the Polish Jews found themselves. Suddenly, they noticed the Gestapo head Baeker striding impatiently down the street, and they drew off to the side to let him pass. His eyes raked them, swept past and then menacingly returned. His gaze was riveted on Inge's muff, and his faced turned red with rage.

"How dare you hold that back!" he screamed.

In a frenzy, he pulled out his revolver and shot the horrified youngster, who collapsed onto the ground. Oblivious to the dead girl who lay silently in blood, the Nazi beast snatched up the muff for which he had murdered her and strode away. White-faced, his heart pounding and aching, Shmuel was left staring down at the motionless body, not knowing what to do. It was the first time someone standing next to him had been shot. Tragically, it would not be the last.

Across the hall from the Rubin family lived Reb Moshe Epstein with his wife and eight children. The official rabbi of the town had left at the outbreak of the war, and Reb Moshe, himself a scholar, had been rendering *halachic* rulings gratis for the Jews of Korczyna. When the economic conditions had worsened, he had begun to take a small stipend to help support his eight children.

In July of 1942, the Judenrat's police warned everyone to get into their houses. The Gestapo had come to town and had ordered that anyone found outside after seven in the evening would be shot. It turned out that the purpose of the curfew was not to keep Jews off the streets, but to have easy access to them in their houses. The Gestapo had marched into the offices of the Judenrat and demanded the names of several people, among them the rabbi of the town. They had been given seven names, one of them was Reb Moshe Epstein. After the hour declared for the curfew, they went around to the houses of the men on the list, arrested them and hauled them off to the lot next to the police station, to be shot. When the Rubins heard gunshots, they assumed the worst. They were confined to their houses all that night, tensely waiting to see what the morning would bring.

Early in the morning, the Polish police knocked on the Epstein door, demanding to know where Reb Moshe was. The answer that he had been arrested the night before was insufficient. The Gestapo, the police bellowed, was looking for him again. When the Polish police had come out in the morning to examine the bodies, they found only six. Reb Moshe was missing. The police chief had phoned Gestapo headquarters in Krosno and had been told that if Reb Moshe was not found within a few hours, they would shoot forty Jews. The Judenrat, too, was ordered to find him.

That night, Shmuel defied the curfew and sneaked outside, where he heard a rumor that Reb Moshe was hiding out at Yanche Infeld's house, not far from the police station. Shmuel stealthily slipped from house to house, working his way over there. When he arrived, he found Reb Moshe in bed, weak from loss of blood. The bullet had grazed him under the ear, and he had fallen down with the other victims. In the middle of the night he fought against his weakness and, despite immense strain, had dragged himself to Infeld's house, where he collapsed.

The Judenrat, too, found out where Reb Moshe was and sent a man to talk to him. Jewish law forbids turning over a Jew to murderers, even to prevent the murder of many others. They asked the rabbi to give himself up in order to prevent the retaliatory murder of forty other Jews.

Every eye in the room turned to the rabbi.

Reb Moshe agreed to their argument. "I am ready to be an atonement for all Israel," he said.

The man from the Judenrat then called the Polish police, who ordered that the prisoner be brought back to the police station. Too weak to walk, Reb Moshe had to be carried on a stretcher, Shmuel supporting one of the poles. How grievous it was to carry a righteous man to his undeserved execution.

When they arrived at the station and Reb Moshe saw the

bodies of the other men who had been shot the night before, his blood boiled. He had one last request, he whispered to the Jews around him. Citing an old custom for burying martyrs, he asked to be buried with a knife in his hand, so that in the future he could personally take revenge on the murderers.

Baeker, in his sick hatred of Jews, and to make sure that no mistakes be made again, had taken the trouble to travel from Krosno to personally perform the execution. His carefully aimed bullet unerringly pierced Reb Moshe's skull as he lay on the stretcher.

Despite the agony of the situation, the Jews worked efficiently, if grimly, to protect the remains of their martyred brethren. Shmuel was becoming initiated in the procedures to take when a fellow Jew is murdered by Nazi brutes. The Jews quickly brought forward a cart and loaded in the bodies, before the Germans would take even the matter of disposal into their own hands. Thus, all seven men received a dignified burial that same day, in accordance with Jewish law, in a common grave. And Reb Moshe's request to be buried with a knife was meticulously fulfilled.

Tishah b'Av, the day of mourning for the destruction of the Temple, followed shortly thereafter. Jews sat on the floor, fasting, and wept as they read of the horrors of the Babylonian conquest, of mothers, starved by the long siege of Jerusalem, who ate their own children; of babes dashed against the rocks by the victors; of sages degraded and young men led away to slavery; of widows weeping for their murdered husbands and of young girls taken captive. They wept as well over the anticipated horrors of their own exile, which was fast approaching. The Jews from the surrounding villages had already been gathered into Korczyna, swelling its Jewish population from eight hundred to sixteen hundred, and the *shtetl* Jews suspected that they, too, would soon be dislodged from their homes.

Krosno was hit first. On Sunday, August 9, the Gestapo ordered all Krosno Jews to report on Monday to the yard next to the train station. The purpose of this procedure, they were cynically told, was "registration." Word was sent to Korczyna Jews who worked in Krosno to stay home on that day. This order applied to Shmuel, who had just recently obtained a "work card."

Despite the orders, however, a few Korczyna Jews sneaked over to Krosno to bring back a report in the evening. The ghastly account was that the Krosno Jews had been kept standing all day in the scorching August sun, without being provided any drinking water. The reports the following day, Tuesday, were yet worse. The suffering victims had been left in the open all Monday night. Tuesday morning, all of them, men, women and children, had been mercilessly beaten by the Gestapo while loaded into closed cattle cars, sixty people to a car.

The only Jews left behind in Krosno were those whose work card exempted them from the "registration" and several hundred others who had decided that it would be wiser to risk evading the order to appear at the train station on Monday. These paid a Pole to ride the train part of the way to see the fate of their brethren. The train headed east, and the Pole stayed with it until its first stop-over. He returned and described the horrible sight. The train cars had been left standing on a siding, while the Jews inside screamed for water with no one answering them. The Pole then told of how one of the Jews, Dr. Baumring, had called out, "Barbarians, that's what you are!" for which the Germans dragged him out and shot him. The Jews of Krosno could only wait in dismay for the next predicament they would have to suffer.

Unfortunately, they did not have long to wait. That same Tuesday, the Gestapo ordered all Jews of Korczyna with jobs to report to their places of work the following day, Wednesday.

Before reporting to the assembly point at six o'clock in the morning, Shmuel took along his *tefillin*, in case he would not be home on the morrow, and exchanged normal good-byes with his mother.

"Go safely and come safely," his mother blessed him, her oldest son. Despite the rumors from Krosno, it did not occur to either of them that she was the one in need of a blessing, nor did they really believe that their ritual parting might indeed be final.

The Korczyna workers were marched to Krosno four abreast, with a police escort, and sent to their places of work. Shmuel's detail fixed the roads and streets. As his team was moved from place to place, it caught occasional glimpses of what went on that day.

Around eleven o'clock, a well-guarded caravan of freight trucks arrived from Korczyna. In the backs of the trucks were all the Jews who had resided in the *shtetl*. Boys and girls, women and babies, old people and invalids, all were crowded together in the trucks, Shmuel's family among them. To avoid outbreaks of violence, many of the Korczyna workers were taken from their jobs and placed under armed guard until the caravan of trucks had reached the train station. Fathers, husbands and sons looked on in helpless fury as their families were driven past. That night, the workers were interned in a camp instead of being sent home to Korczyna.

The trucks discharged their "freight" in the train station and drove off to other *shtetls* in the region to collect more deportees. All Jews over fifty were separated from the others and sent away the same day. The others were left sitting on the ground for two days, after which they, too, were stuffed into freight cars and carried away. The three-hundred-year-old community of Korczyna was gone.

CRACOW, POLAND • 1942

A few weeks later, Shmuel and several other workers from Korczyna were moved to a labor camp on the outskirts of Cracow. There, they had to help build their own prison and surround it with a double wall of electrified barbed wire. Construction began in the middle of 1942, on land adjacent to the Jewish cemetery, and was extended into the territory of the cemetery proper. Rocks from the cemetery walls were used, as well as gravestones, to help construct the foundations of the buildings and roads. Shmuel was attached to the Barrackenbau, the groups of unskilled laborers assigned to put up enough barracks to hold the Jews of Cracow who were pushed out of their ghetto homes. Since the construction under private contractors was going too slow for the SS, it had set up a "Building Office" in the camp, staffed by Jewish engineers from the ghetto. Once the SS could punish construction delays by whipping the supervisors, the work pace quickened considerably.

However, Shmuel's transfer to Cracow, and the searches which accompanied it, marked the beginning of a series of daily victories of Shmuel Rubin over his captors.

The peak moments of danger were the constant inspections. The prisoners' bodies, their clothes, their bundles of possessions, their barracks, were continually being searched for contraband. Shmuel managed to keep possession of his *tefillin* through the help of his friends and the fact that the guards could not search everyone and everywhere at the same time. When they were being inspected, the package was set down casually somewhere on the barrack's floor. If the Jews were in transit and were subjected to a body search, they would pass the bundle from one row to another. If their possessions were being searched, they carried the bundle on their persons.

Keeping possession of the *tefillin* was one thing, finding the time and privacy to put them on once a day was another. The most dangerous part of the procedure was winding the leather strap around the left arm seven times. Once that was done, the straps, as well as the cube placed on the biceps, could be hidden by a shirt sleeve. A cap could hide the leather cube worn on the head. Of course, one still had to hope that there would not be a surprise inspection, since the first order given was often, "Hats off!"

The best time for putting on *tefillin* was early in the morning, before the guards woke up, but it was not always possible. The guards were up quite early, and understandably, Shmuel often slept with the soundness one would expect from a fifteen-year-old boy exhausted by daily twelve-hour shifts of hard labor. If his work assignment was inside the camp, he could take his *tefillin* along and try to put them on during the lunch break. If his detail was working outside, the searches at the gate made that too dangerous; then he would just have to wait until the team was back in their barracks and everyone else had gone to bed. But one way or another, Shmuel's luck always held. Every day, whether morning, noon or evening, he managed to find a short stretch of time in which to put on his *tefillin* without being caught.

Eventually, Shmuel was moved to Plaszow, another camp, where putting on *tefillin* was even more dangerous.

When the Cracow ghetto was liquidated in March of 1943, the 10,000 Jews judged fit for labor were transferred to Plaszow. Some of their ghetto enterprises were transferred with them as well, among which was the paper works, including a printing house that turned out Nazi propaganda leaflets. The paper works also served as a refuge for the distinguished elders of the Cracow religious community.

One morning, a German guard passed by the window of the paper works and spotted three Jews wearing their *tefillin* and praying. He jumped through the window, wrapped the straps of their *tefillin* around their necks and dragged them, struggling and choking, through the streets of the camp. He continued forward with his gagging victims until he reached the open mass graves at the site that had come to be known, quite appropriately, as "Death Hill." There he cold-bloodedly shot all three Jews and dumped their bodies into the grave.

Putting on *tefillin* was only one of the religious duties that Shmuel and his friends were determined to undertake. With the approach of spring came the problem of food on *Pesach*. The mainstay of the prison camp diet was bread, which Shmuel and his friends wanted to avoid eating during the eight days of *Pesach*. They would have to find some other source of nourishment, or they would all starve. The solution came in the form of a friend who worked as a supplier to the kitchen. Every time he unloaded a potato sack, he managed to pocket one potato, which was then carefully transferred to a hole the boys dug in an inconspicuous spot. It was a very hunger-filled *Pesach*, but the boys did manage to get through the holiday without eating anything leavened.

Shmuel was never caught in his *tefillin* nor apprehended with the stolen potatoes during *Pesach*. When his turn finally came to stand on "Death Hill" and face a loaded revolver, it was for a more commonplace, less heroic offense. To understand why his "crime" was serious enough to warrant a sentence of death, it is necessary to know more about Plaszow and its commander, Ammon Goett.

In February, 1943, command of Plaszow was given to *Untersturmfuehrer* Ammon Goett, who had served his apprenticeship for the position in the fiendish extermination camps of Belzec, Treblinka and Sobibor. Goett was a cold-blooded murderer whose ghoulishly nonchalant attitude towards rendering people lifeless was augmented by his sick pride in his marksmanship. One day, while speaking to a contractor in his office, he glanced through the window and noticed some worker who seemed to be leaning on his shovel. Pulling out his revolver, Goett took aim and killed the prisoner with a single shot. Then he returned to the conversation.

Goett's two goals in life were to live in luxury and to avoid being sent to the front. He believed that the more productive his camp would appear, the more he would achieve his aims. He utilized several methods to push through expansion of the camp at a dizzying pace. One was splitting the construction workers into day and night shifts. Another method was one he had learned through his training in the death camps, where he had witnessed Jews dying by the thousands. It taught him that torturing and killing Jews led to more efficient work by those kept alive, even if they were given only minimal sustenance.

Having received from his predecessor a nearly empty camp, Goett filled it by liquidating the ghettos of Cracow and Tarnov. In his infernal sense of efficiency, those considered unfit for work, primarily women and children, were mercilessly killed or transported to extermination camps. Goett himself murdered fifty women from Tarnov who were caught concealing their babies in their backpacks. First he killed the children in front of their mothers, then he had the women brought forward, and he personally shot them, in groups of four. When he had finished, he wiped the sweat from his forehead and called for a basin of water in which to wash his hands.

It was necessary that the camp contain the largest possible number of war-related factories, in order to make it seem to Goett's superiors like a project worth the materials and manpower invested in it. The actual quality and quantity of production from those factories was not particularly important to Goett because he could easily fool the periodic inspection parties or bribe them with the jewels and valuables confiscated during the liquidation of the ghetto. Of course, most of these riches had gone into Goett's personal coffers rather than those of the SS, and the Jews in the camp knew about this all too well.

The factories and inmates of the camp were divided according to two distinct levels of productivity and efficiency. Whereas for those employed in work connected with the war effort there was a very low standard to be met, for those connected with the actual building of the camp, the *Barrackenbau*, there was a much higher standard. Shmuel had the misfortune to be placed on the *Barrackenbau*.

It did not only involve the most difficult work in the camp, it was also the most dangerous. If the work was not completed on schedule, Goett did not content himself with threatening to kill the supervisor of a project or hostages from his family. He also shot a few workers whom he judged to be slacking, and thereafter the others worked more vigorously. The regular murders became so commonplace that groups of workers coming back from a project would numbly exchange scores as if they had been attending a soccer match. "6 to 0," they would say, "8 to 0," or "10 to 0," meaning six, eight, or ten people had been killed during the shift to encourage the others to work harder.

Set on a rise overlooking the camp was Goett's private villa on SS Street. The complex contained a large kennel for Goett's pack of killer dogs, a spacious house and a heavily guarded wall. The prisoners avoided the villa as much as possible.

During the paving of "Industry Street," rock chips for the foundations had to be brought by wagon from the quarry near "Death Hill" over railway track that led up the slope of SS Street, past the villas of the overlords. However, the engine to pull the wagons was never delivered. This deficiency engendered one of the crueler innovations of Plaszow, namely, a train pulled by human beings. Three attached wagons were loaded with stones, and long ropes were tied to either side of the first car. Thirty-five women were lined up along each of the ropes and were forced to drag the train forward in step—one, two, three, four, one, two, three, four. The human train was kept running up the slope day and night, fifty-five torturous minutes to each circuit.

One night, as the freezing women, dressed in rags and blankets, were hauling the heavy wagons up the grade, they encountered an unwelcome audience. Goett had been giving a party in his villa for his fashionable friends from outside the camp. The building was brightly lit, filled with gay celebrants in furs and evening clothes. Goett proudly led a glittering procession of his guests out into the foggy night, toward the sound of the guards calling, "One, two, three, four." To his warped mind, his guests, especially the pretty ladies, would be impressed by his creativity.

The wind was sharp, and some of the more delicate guests were wrapping their furs more tightly around themselves, when they beheld the tortured women pulling the stone-laden wagons, the coarse ropes clutched in their frozen hands. The tipsy chatter of the guests stilled and they fell silent, staring at the dismal procession which had materialized out of the darkness. Only the whistle of the wind and the shouts of the guards cut through the chill air.

One of Goett's favorites whispered in his ear, revealing to the conscienceless brute that the sight of the wretched women was having an undesirable effect on his entourage. Choosing an uncharacteristic pose of magnanimity, he called out to the guards to have the wagons braked and allow the women to return to the barracks instead of completing the night shift. It was a surprise to the tormented women, but a very welcome one.

The day Shmuel himself was led off to "Death Hill" began as any normal day in a Nazi labor camp. Breakfast consisted of coffee and an insufficient amount of bread. The prisoners then set off for their work assignments in groups of fifty, each group under the care of its own *kapo*. The men were carefully counted before being allowed through the gate in the fence surrounding the residence compound, and the *kapo* was responsible for accounting for all of them when he brought them back in the evening. No expense or effort was spared to prevent even a single Jew from escaping. Electrified barbed wire fences circled various sections of the camp, in addition to the two large perimeter fences with the guard towers. At the daily peak moment of danger—Goett's morning inspection—he walked from project to project, checking to see how much was being accomplished.

On this particular day, Shmuel did not notice the officer's approach in time to pursue his job with extra vigor. By the time he heard the snap of Goett's voice upbraiding him, it was already too late. Ten Jews, Shmuel among them, were accused of slacking, and they were sentenced to execution on "Death Hill." Goett called two guards, and they marched the ten men over to that fearful spot.

The prisoners were ordered to undress and then were arranged in a line with Shmuel at one end. Goett, an enormous man, over six and a half feet tall and weighing two hundred fifty pounds, stood facing them, impatiently waiting for the preliminaries to be over so that he could get on with the execution. Drawing his revolver, he began to fire, starting from the beginning of the line. This time, not one but nine people would be shot from Shmuel's side, and this time he, too, would face the gun. One man dead. Two. Three. Four. Five. Six. Seven. Eight. One by one, his comrades crumpled dead to the ground. The ninth shot was fired, and only Shmuel was left standing. The gun barrel swerved toward Shmuel, the murderer squeezed the trigger.

Nothing happened. The gun did not fire.

Goett stared down at his revolver. It was always dependable, and this malfunction surprised him. But nothing would faze him, and nothing would deter his aims. If the gun could not kill the Jew one way, it would another. Flipping it in the air and catching it by its barrel, he strode forward to where the deathly frightened boy was standing and raised it, butt first, high in the air. As he reached Shmuel, he brought the gun smashing down in a long arc to the side of the boy's head, putting in the blow all the force of his huge body. The gun butt struck Shmuel's jaw, knocking out several teeth, and broke his collarbone.

But he was still conscious.

Goett looked down at the bleeding boy, lying in a heap on the ground but somehow still alive. A new use for this unusually resilient boy took form in the villain's egoistic mind.

"You have luck," he said grudgingly. "You come home with me."

Shmuel, writhing in pain, slowly picked himself up and followed Goett to his villa a few hundred meters away.

"You will guard the house until you recover," Goett told him when they arrived.

Shmuel was retained as his would-be murderer's house guard for two weeks, until he was well enough to return to work.

Three separate miracles combined to save Shmuel from a seemingly inevitable execution, each of them a necessary component. The misfired shot or the ill-aimed blow, each by itself, would have been enough cause for Shmuel to thank G-d for His special protection. The third miracle, to be kept alive as Goett's own lucky charm, was the most ironic and astounding one of all.

In the summer of 1944, Goett's superiors in the SS discovered his embezzlement from the SS of huge sums of Jewish money and his selling, on the black market, of supplies intended for the camp. He escaped the Gestapo, but was finally captured by the Russians after they conquered Poland. He was tried by the Poles in 1946, condemned to death and executed by hanging.

Baeker, the Gestapo chief in Krosno, remained free after the war. He was arrested in 1964, pleaded insanity and was confined to a mental hospital. He was finally brought to trial in 1973, more than thirty years after the destruction of Korczyna and Krosno. Shmuel, who answered a notice in the papers requesting witnesses, was flown to Bonn to testify about the murders of Inge and of Reb Moshe Epstein. Baeker was sentenced to death and executed. Shmuel was the living extension of the knife Reb Moshe had taken with him to his grave.

Shmuel was the only member of his family to survive the war. After passing through Korczyna, where he helped place a marker on Reb Moshe's grave, he reached Israel. In the course of time, he recuperated both mentally and physically and married into the family of the founder of Bnei Brak. Shmuel took a responsible position in the city's administration, and he and his wife raised several children. At each celebration, birthday, *bar-mitzvah* or wedding, he marvels again, "To think that I would have had children and would have survived to see an occasion like this!"

The central portion of the forest fire is subsiding for lack of fuel, but the blaze continues to spread in an ever-widening circle. The flames reach one of the oldest and tallest trees in the woods. It stands wreathed in smoke, its lower branches burning and its foliage on fire from foot to tip. The flames eat into the trunk, and finally, with a loud snap, the whole tree leans majestically to one side and begins to fall. The tip describes a wide arc through the air, slams into a young sapling not yet engulfed by the flames and snaps its trunk in two. But the top of the sapling, with its full load of seed, is knocked into a forest stream and saved from the fire.

WATERS OF RESCUE 3

The Jewish community of Hamburg was an ancient and proud one. Its destruction was a work of years, and Avraham Rosenkranz was an unwilling witness to every step of the agonizing process.

Though born in Denmark, Mr. Rosenkranz had studied at a Jewish teachers' seminary in Hanover and had taken a position in the Talmud Torah of Hamburg, an institution with a hundred-and-fifty-year history. He had taught there for twenty-odd years, and many of the community's younger members had been his students. All of his fourteen children, though they inherited his Danish citizenship, had been born in Hamburg. The family felt itself at home in the Hamburg Jewish community. But that home became much less homelike with the rise of the Nazis and the unwelcome surveillance of the Jewish community by the secret police.

Mr. Rosenkranz turned his eyes toward Denmark as a

possible port of refuge. In 1938, he sent his oldest son Leo to Copenhagen, knowing that if the boy remained a resident in Germany past his twenty-first birthday, he would forfeit his Danish citizenship.

One afternoon soon after Leo left, there was a sharp rap on the door. One of the children opened it, and in stepped two men from the fearful Gestapo, demanding to see the man of the house. Mr. Rosenkranz emerged from his study, and the policemen began interrogating him in brusque tones about the purpose of Leo's trip.

In the middle of the questioning, there was a further knock on the door. Two of the children opened it, finding one of their father's fellow teachers standing outside in the stairwell. They waved him off, whispering frantically, "Go away, go away. The Gestapo is here." The man beat a hasty retreat. There was also a relative staying with them, but fortunately, he was unaware of the happenings and remained locked in his room. To the family's relief, the secret police left without having found anything particularly incriminating.

A few months later, on November 10, 1938, came *Kristallnacht.* As part of that terror's aftermath, in addition to the internment of Jewish teachers and the destruction of almost all synagogues, the Jewish students were expelled from the German schools. At first, this caused a stream of new students from the provinces to arrive in cities which, like Hamburg, had functioning Jewish schools. The Talmud Torah therefore opened special classes for students with weak Jewish backgrounds. Soon, however, the classrooms began to empty again as more and more Jewish children emigrated from Germany to other European countries. Both the Nazi government and the Jewish parents were pushing that emigration as hard as possible. Only the difficulty of obtaining visas kept the classes in the Talmud Torah from emptying yet faster. As the school-age population dropped, the boys' and girls' schools were thrown together, with only one class per grade.

The uncomfortable attention paid by the Gestapo to Mr. Rosenkranz increased. One day, while he was at the school, two Gestapo men came to his apartment and demanded that Mrs. Rosenkranz show them his documents. Mrs. Rosenkranz unlocked her husband's roll-top desk and began a frantic search for them. As if things were not already tense enough, another luckless situation developed. Little Minna, a toddler, knowing nothing about the Nazis or the Gestapo, wobbled over to the two policemen and began tugging at their trouser legs, as the older children were desperately trying to convince the men that they honestly did not know the location of their father's documents. The children, terrified that the men would grow annoyed at Minna and do her some harm, tried to call her away. But she clung stubbornly to her position. Evidently, the arguing was intense enough to keep the savages distracted from the girl, and double relief encompassed the Rosenkranz family when the men gave up and stalked out of the room.

Mr. Rosenkranz continued his own private emigration effort, transferring his children to Copenhagen as fast as he could find benefactors willing to take them in. By the spring of 1941, only seven of the fourteen children were still living at home, and he decided that it was time to arrange for their send-off as well as his wife's. He preferred to remain in Hamburg, meanwhile, for two reasons. He had a tax debt to pay off before he would be allowed to leave, and he preferred not to give up his teacher's post voluntarily. He did not want to have any complaints of desertion lodged against him later.

It took five months and considerable pressure to obtain the necessary documents. Havens for three more children had been found, leaving only four more and Mrs. Rosenkranz still home. By that time, the situation of the Jews in Germany had worsened considerably, and Mr. Rosenkranz wished that he himself also had documents by which to leave with his family. However, he still did not apply for a permit before the rest of his family was off German soil, out of fear that doing so might jeopardize them.

In October, a thousand Hamburg Jews were "evacuated" to the ghetto in Polish Lodz, followed soon after by another two thousand to Minsk and Riga. All property of the evacuees was confiscated, and they were allowed only fifty kilograms of baggage. Friends slated for deportation would call on the Rosenkranz family to say good-bye and leave objects of sentimental value for safekeeping, hoping to come back for them after the war. The many tearful partings weighed very heavily on Mrs. Rosenkranz. The permits for Mrs. Rosenkranz and the four remaining children finally arrived in November, and at the end of the month, she set out for Copenhagen together with the four children.

The very next day, Mr. Rosenkranz submitted an application for his own permit. As he feared, his application was not acted upon, and applications by his brother in Copenhagen to the foreign ministry there were also rejected. No reason was given, but finally, through some friends with connections, his brother managed to discover the problem. It seems he had once been arrested by the Gestapo. Mr. Rosenkranz felt that the ministry did him too much "honor." His arrest consisted of once having been called in by the Gestapo to explain the contents of a school notebook found among some primers he had sent to Copenhagen. That hardly branded him as a criminal too dangerous to be allowed to travel abroad. All remonstrances, however, did not produce the needed travel permits.

The Jews still in Germany remained in suspense about the fate of those deported to the ghettos. Censored postcards arrived from the East, but these were too short to convey much information. Mr. Rosenkranz received a request from the grandmother of a former student at the school, asking for a copy of her granddaughter's graduation certificate, in the hope that this document might help her in her new home. Did that mean the deportees would be allowed to lead relatively normal lives within the confines of the ghettos? A group of teachers and students being deported to Minsk, asked permission from the Gestapo to take books and workbooks with them to Minsk, with the aim of reorganizing the school there. Permission to take along a hundred kilograms of books was granted. Mr. Rosenkranz, serving in November as the Talmud Torah's acting principal, wrote to a publishing house in Leipzig to order more books sent to the group in Minsk, but received a polite refusal on the grounds that export regulations would not permit such a shipment.

The government promised that students studying away from home would be reunited with their families when they arrived in the East. How much reliance could one place on such promises? One father, at least, was dubious. In March, he wrote to Dr. Jonas, the principal of the Talmud Torah in Hamburg, saying that he would not send his son back to the school for fear that the boy would not manage to rejoin the family on their way to "agricultural labor" in Lublin, Poland.

Even before the deportations from Hamburg had begun, Dr. Jonas had decided that he would try to run the school as if conditions were normal, and he continued to work in that spirit throughout the year, adjusting as well as possible to the occasional sudden deportations of groups of students and of teachers. At the end of the year, as at the end of every year, he scheduled registration of new students for the first grade to take place from June 15 to July 1, 1942.

On May 31, all the electric equipment belonging to the Jewish Community Offices was confiscated, and Dr. Plaut, the leader of the community, called in Mr. Rosenkranz to help with the formalities. During the task, Dr. Plaut came over to Rosenkranz's desk.

"You don't have to go in to school tomorrow," Plaut said casually. After a pause, he continued, "You don't have to go in any more at all."

"Don't make bad jokes," responded Mr. Rosenkranz.

"Come over to my office," Plaut replied, "and I will show you black on white."

To his horror, Mr. Rosenkranz discovered that all Jewish schools in the Reich were to be closed as of the next day, June 1, and that all teachers were forbidden to give private lessons. It was forbidden to teach a Jewish child anything at all. This was a terrible blow. Until then, no matter how dark things looked, there was hope for the future through the children. Now the blackness was closing in around the next generation as well. Mr. Rosenkranz was not the only Jew to be shocked, and he considered it an honorable statement of German Jewry that no decree of the government had shaken and disturbed it as much as this one had.

The school staff members were not actually sent away immediately. They were given a month in which to prepare certificates for departing pupils, to return travel permits granted to some of the teachers and students, to evacuate the school buildings, to inventory the equipment and to estimate its value. The students, too, were not left idle for long.

The evacuations to the East were reintroduced, and on July 11, the students were made part of a large transport to the unspeakable nightmare known as Auschwitz. Through devious Nazi efficiency, Dr. Jonas and Mr. Rosenkranz were kept busy with administrative details, while their students, their life's work, were shipped off to a horrid, deadly fate. Dr. Jonas labored for the first two weeks of July preparing estimates of the value of the school equipment. On July 16, there was a second transport, mostly of older people, to the "model" concentration camp in Theresienstadt, the camp kept on display for visitors. On July 19 came the third and final transport, and with it the final blow to the Talmud Torah—the principal Dr. Jonas was among the deportees.

The last steps in sending the school equipment to the Ministry of Education were taken by Mr. Rosenkranz himself. Everything was gone, including desks, books, students, teachers, principal. The school record books had been kept in good order since 1805, when the Talmud Torah had been founded by the grandfather of Rabbi Samson Rafael Hirsch. They recorded a century and a half of dedication to Jewish education. The final entry was made by Mr. Rosenkranz on July 13, 1942.

Mr. Rosenkranz refused to accept the decree against teaching. As long as there are Jewish children and a teacher for them, Jewish education would have to go on. Heroically, despite the danger involved, he gave lessons in the morning to four children who remained in town.

The religious life of the community also continued. Most of the Jews left in town were "protected" either by mixed marriage or by citizenship in an allied country such as Hungary or Romania. Prayer services continued to be held daily, though filling the quota of ten men depended upon the assistance of partners in mixed marriages. The community even built a *mikveh*, a ritual bath, after the former one was closed by the government. The materials were purchased with "black" money, and all the construction took place under cover of darkness. Mr. Rosenkranz wrote a poem in Hebrew to commemorate the *mikveh's* completion and left a copy in the facility's wall. The *mikveh* was actually constructed for use by one individual woman, and it was finished on the holiday of *Tu b'Shvat*, at the beginning of 1943. So passed the last days of the ancient community of Hamburg.

COPENHAGEN, DENMARK • 1943

S pring came to Copenhagen. Brightly colored blossoms filled up window boxes along the neat Danish streets. When the King of Denmark made his daily ride on horseback, he passed beds of spring flowers and lakes graced by ducks and swans. As he rode past the corner of Ole Suhr Street, he reined in his horse slightly and nodded to the rabbi of Machzikei Hadas Synagogue, who had come out to honor the mortal king, as a way of doing honor to the King of kings. Without the special protection of the Danish king, the lot of the Jews in German-occupied Denmark would have been much worse than it was. The third anniversary of the German conquest was approaching, but the Jews of Denmark still enjoyed all the privileges of full Danish citizenship.

Spring came at last for the Rosenkranz family as well, with the news that their father would finally be allowed to join them. The winter had been very hard on Mrs. Rosenkranz, and many nights she had sat next to the small, inadequate stove, crying in worry over the fate of her husband and their friends from Hamburg. She and the children had been living on the charity of the community, donations by her husband's relatives, and the small earnings of the grown children. She did not even have enough plates on which to serve the meager rations to her hungry children. The apartment was so small that in order to provide a modicum of floor space in the apartment, the children had to sleep in triple-decker beds. The classes in school were given in the country's tongue, Danish, and this only increased the children's troubles, since some of them had already lost a year of school. While most of these problems would not vanish with the arrival of her husband, they would be much easier to bear once she knew he was safe and once he began sharing them.

Mrs. Rosenkranz took only a few of the older children with

her to meet the train, since it was never practical to travel with the entire brood. When Mr. Rosenkranz descended from the train, the children barely recognized him. Not only was he terribly thin, but he seemed to have aged much more than the four years that had passed since they had last seen him. During the taxi ride home, Mr. Rosenkranz did not speak much about his experiences.

The older sisters, who had stayed home to babysit, had prepared a reception. All the children were arranged in a line, and as soon as they caught sight of their father, they began to sing, "*Shalom Aleichem* . . . " Mr. Rosenkranz still did not say much, but he was deeply touched. After all these years of separation, to have all sixteen members of the family together again was almost unbelievable.

Mr. Rosenkranz and his family became members of the synagogue on Ole Suhr Street, where the level of observance, among young people as well as among their elders, was quite high. The synagogue building, a converted townhouse, was usually crowded, occupied by fifty-odd large families, mostly of Eastern European origin. Things were relatively calm, although every morning, on their way into the synagogue, Mr. Rosenkranz and his sons walked past a German guard, since the school next door had been taken over by the Germans for use as a military post.

However, the relative calm of the spring and summer ended abruptly in August, 1943. The relentless Germans staged a coup, deposed and imprisoned the king and placed their own man at the head of the government. The school next to the synagogue was given over for the Gestapo's use, and now a black-uniformed soldier stood guard at the door, glaring at the Jews as they walked past toward their morning prayers.

The main office of the Jewish community, centered around the big synagogue downtown, was required to turn over to the

Gestapo a list of addresses of all Jews in Denmark. The Jews, very nervous by these and similar moves, were nevertheless advised by Danes in responsible positions to refrain from organizing any mass evacuation to neighboring Sweden, for fear it would precipitate countermoves by the Gestapo. A few of the wealthier Jews, fearing confiscation of property, did pack up and quietly move to Sweden, but most Jews sat tight in Copenhagen and waited to see what would transpire.

Summer drew to a close, and the Jewish New Year approached. For the week preceding *Rosh Hashanah*, the members of the synagogue on Ole Suhr Street came early for the special penitential prayer, recited this year with particular fervor, in light of the dangerous political situation. The prayers of the day before *Rosh Hashanah* are particularly long, and the service started quite early. The rabbi spoke quietly to each person individually, telling him word had just been sent over from the main community offices about a Gestapo raid expected in the next few days. Ships were already waiting in the harbor to carry prisoners to concentration camps in Eastern Europe. Everyone was advised to take cover immediately with Christian families and to stay out of their homes over the holiday.

Meanwhile, Mrs. Rosenkranz and her daughters, not yet having heard the terrible news, were bustling about, preparing for *Rosh Hashanah*. When Mr. Rosenkranz returned home from the morning prayers, he found the house filled with a fresh aroma of baking, and everything spic and span. The irony of it all struck him, especially when he glanced at the letter on the hall table, saying that his daughter Rosa had been accepted to the vocational high school she dreamed of attending and could start her studies on Monday. How easily a dream could collapse! By Monday, Rosa might be on her way to Poland in the hold of a ship, unless he could find hiding places for her and the other children. The three oldest boys happened to be safely away in the countryside, but how was he to find Christian foster homes for his other eleven dark-haired children? It had been enough when he had to find Jewish foster homes for the ten he had originally sent ahead to Copenhagen from Hamburg. Almost the only acquaintance he had among the Gentiles was Mr. Larking, who lived across the hall. But Mr. Larking's brother was a volunteer in the SS, which hardly seemed to make him a likely provider of refuge. Who else was there? Mr. Rosenkranz allowed the women to continue their holiday preparations undisturbed, while he tried to think of some way to save his family.

Fortunately for the Rosekranzes, other members of the community did have more connections among the Gentiles. David, a veterinary student, went straight from the synagogue to his university building, where he began contacting the professors and enlisting their help. The teachers began organizing immediately, preparing lists of faculty members who could take Jews into their homes. David then went on from there and appealed to the principal and teachers of his old school, Christianshavn High School, in the suburb of Lyngby. They agreed to help him hide Jews who had no immediate contacts of their own in Gentile circles. Thus it was that, by the afternoon, people began knocking on the Rosenkranz door to take away children, one or two at a time, and the Rosenkranz family members were distributed to a number of Lyngby houses. Only the older boys, who had gone into hiding with connections from their jobs, were located elsewhere.

Rosa and Daniel left together to their protectors, carrying only a tiny bundle of things, to avoid looking conspicuous while walking through the streets. As Rosa walked out the door, she cast a last, sad glance back at the apartment. On the side table lay her acceptance letter to high school; the dining-room table was already set for the *Rosh Hashanah* dinner they would never eat, set with the white tablecloth, the long rows of plates and silverware, the neatly folded white napkins. Something seemed to shift inside her. From this moment on, she would know that such things as plates and glasses were not important in the least.

Rosa and Daniel were billeted with a teacher from David's school, Mr. Aage Bertelsen. The Danish family was very kind to them and did their best to deal with the intricacies of a kosher diet. The vegetables and bread that the children could eat were quite a disappointment when compared to the delicious holiday meal the Rosenkranz family had abandoned, but they appreciated the good will of their hosts in accommodating what seemed to the Danes like a very peculiar diet. The foster children were advertised as distant cousins to the neighborhood children, and they stayed indoors, since the story would not stand many people's scrutiny if they saw the youngsters' dark hair. Their hosts' two young children were in on the secret and took part in the cover-up.

Mr. Rosenkranz was hosted by a Mr. Prior. He would have liked to visit his children to know how they were settled and how they were managing to obtain kosher food, but his appearance was too Jewish for him to be safe out on the streets. In addition, no one wanted to alert the Gestapo by having Jews seen in the streets in unusual places. The Gestapo had not yet made the threatened raid and were still under the impression that the Jews were sitting quietly in their homes, available for easy capture.

Rosh Hashanah fell on Thursday and Friday that year, followed immediately by *Shabbos*. The Jews had only Wednesday morning and afternoon in which to take cover, followed by a three-day period in which all but life-saving activities were religiously curtailed. Therefore, although the organizers of the rescue mission, such as David, were using the telephone, for the Rosenkranz family there was nothing to do but sit quietly and wait. The hosts carried messages from one fragment of the family to another, and Mr. Bertelsen came over to meet Mr. Rosenkranz and assure him that Rosa and her brother were in good hands, but in general each group was quite isolated. The expected raid did not materialize on Wednesday night or even on Thursday night, and Mr. Rosenkranz began to wonder if the whole alarm had perhaps been empty noise.

The Gestapo made its raid on Friday night. The thugs broke into home after home, only to find that the inhabitants had already fled. Of the seven thousand Jews they were pursuing, they netted only four hundred and fifty on the first night, upon whom, however, they vented their frustration. Early Saturday morning, Mr. Bertelsen visited the local Danish police chief, who was also in sympathy with the efforts to rescue the Jews. The officer had just received reports on the raid from two of his men patrolling the coastal area, and Mr. Bertelsen found him shaken by the cruelty with which the German police had treated those Jews they had captured along the shore.

The Danish hosts in Lyngby took counsel and decided to have "their" Jews fill out Swedish visa application forms. A German-Jewish acquaintance had informed them that in Germany the Gestapo had occasionally allowed legal emigration immediately after a raid. Mr. Bertelsen undertook the project of distributing the forms, which were picked up and returned by the Jews' hosts. Rosa and Daniel were kept out of sight, in case one of the callers should turn out to be coming for some other purpose. Once, though, they were called out of hiding, in order to convince a suspicious caller that Mr. Bertelsen was not a Gestapo agent in disguise.

Sunday afternoon, David came by to check on the success of the "visa office," which had already collected fifty completed forms. He had been called up into the Danish civil defense organization, and his blue uniform allowed him relative freedom of travel, even after curfew hours. Of course, his thick black beard did render his appearance a bit suspicious, but eventually, the Bertelsens located an electric razor, and David shaved off the stubble. For many of the Lyngby hosts, this rescue operation afforded them their first contact with strictly Orthodox Jews, and they reacted with a mixture of exasperation and respect when faced with restrictions such as the prohibition against shaving with a straight razor.

Already by Sunday, when it was no longer "immediately after a raid," Mr. Bertelsen and his friends were beginning to despair of arranging legal emigration to Sweden, and they began to look into the possibilities of illegal transport. They located one group, which operated out of the university, but their routes were full of passengers at the time.

With the three-day Jewish holiday over that Sunday, Mr. Rosenkranz also went into action. His most pressing problem was arranging the finances to smuggle sixteen people into Sweden, which would cost at least a hundred dollars per person. He decided to risk contacting Mr. Larking, the man whose apartment was across the hall from the Rosenkranz's, despite his brother's having served in the SS. Mr. Rosenkranz could not visit him in Copenhagen, since it was still too dangerous for him to appear on the streets, nor could he discuss this subject on the phone openly. He therefore called up the former neighbor and discreetly asked him to come for a visit at the Priors, his hosts in Lyngby.

Mr. Larking, a retired acrobat who ran a second-hand store, turned out to be very sympathetic to the plight of the Jews, despite his brother's leanings. He promised to raise as much money as he could by selling the items the Rosenkranz family had abandoned in their apartment. David's family, too, eventually consigned their possessions to Mr. Larking, intending to use the proceeds to help Jews who could not otherwise obtain money to pay for their passage.

Selling second-hand furniture is a slow business, though, and most of the money to help Jews who could not pay their own fare came not through sales but outright donations given by the Danes. Mr. Bertelsen, in his memoirs of the period, tells of one remarkable instance of the Danes' willingness to contribute, which occurred while he was travelling with David and Mr. Prior. The three were speaking about the rescue efforts, but in tones they thought were too low to be heard by anyone else on the subway train.

Suddenly, a woman in the car got up from her seat, went over to Mr. Bertelsen and asked, "Would you like some money?"

"Yes, thank you very much," he replied at once.

She took out her wallet and gave him all the bills it contained, then returned to her seat without further comment. That was the spirit which kept a steady stream of money flowing into the coffers of the underground rescue organization.

On Monday, David's sister called from the coast. The night before, she had unsuccessfully attempted to get across to Sweden on a boat she heard was making a clandestine trip from Elsinore. However, she had now been offered a place on a transport leaving that evening from the town of Humlebaek, and she was told that it could take some fifty of the Lyngby Jews as well. Mr. Prior arranged to collect the whole Rosenkranz family in a car, while Mr. Bertelsen and his friends took several other groups, each by a different route. When the Rosenkranz family arrived in Humlebaek, they were assigned to one of the houses near the station, all of which were crowded with refugee Jews.

Late that night, a message arrived that the Gestapo was searching the houses along the coast, so the Lyngby group, with the Rosenkranz family included, moved to a hayloft a little way in from the coast. Some fifty people in all made themselves beds with the straw as both mattress and coverlet and fell asleep.

The following day dragged on with nothing for the refugees

to do but wait quietly in the drafty loft to see what the evening would bring. A Danish women's organization took care of sending up food to the refugees. One of the Danes watching over the group engaged Rosa and another child in a game of cards just to keep them occupied. He seemed surprised that they could relax enough to enjoy it. The Danes organizing the rescue operation felt the responsibility of other people's lives resting very heavily on their shoulders.

The Rosenkranz family and the others waited in the loft for two days. On Wednesday night, two trucks were brought around, and the Jews were loaded in, lifted over the sideboards or backboards of the trucks as if they were sacks of flour and placed crouching or flat in the bottom of the truck. They had to remain low so that their heads would not show over the truck's sideboards. The whole operation took place in silence, without complaints. The half moon was just rising as the trucks pulled out of the barn and started on the road for Elsinore, where a number of fishing-craft were supposed to be waiting for them.

Eventually, the trucks stopped, and two of the Danes got out of the cabs and entered a house. There was a muffled sound of a somewhat heated discussion, and then Mr. Bertelsen came out of the house and around to the back of the trucks to explain the situation. Instead of the eleven boats they had been expecting, there was a sole fishing cutter reserved for them. Mr. Bertelsen suggested that since the Rosenkranz family had the most children, they should be the ones to go, and no one objected to the idea. There even turned out to be room for another family of three.

The party, sixteen in all, was led through a garden and out onto a narrow bridge which led to the shore. The last section of the bridge was actually a pier in the water, leading out to where the boats were tied. Young Elsie Rosenkranz was following her youngest sister, six-year-old Minna, when it seemed to her that the little girl was about to lose her balance. Elsie leaned forward to show her what to hold on to, lost her own balance and fell into the water. Fortunately, it was only a couple of feet deep at that point, but that was enough to get her clothing thoroughly soaked before one of the Danish helpers managed to fish her out. The rest of the family was loaded into small rowboats without incident and rowed out to the fishing cutter.

Elsie was wrapped in blankets and spent the trip huddled on her father's knee. The other children also stayed down in the boat for protection against the cold.

Once or twice during the trip, the motor had to be shut off to avoid being heard by German patrol boats, but in general, the trip was blessedly uneventful. Toward the end of the journey, the children went up on deck, from which they saw the jeweled lights of Sweden stretching across the shore.

After years of living in a blacked-out country, to be seeing such a dazzling sight seemed to them as gazing at a fairyland, and they were so elated that they proceeded to sing the Swedish national anthem.

The boys Leo and Joseph were soon found to have safely arrived with another group of escapees, and Mr. Rosenkranz was confident that Max, too, would soon get across in sound condition. After spending Thursday night in a refugee shelter that lacked kosher food, Mr. Rosenkranz got hold of the address of a synagogue where a number of people from his home congregation planned to spend the coming *Yom Kippur*. The whole family set out on *Erev Yom Kippur*, rather hungry, on a three-hour train ride.

The afternoon was wearing on, and once the sun set, it would be forbidden for them to carry their bundles, not to mention to eat or drink. Finally, Mr. Rosenkranz managed to flag two taxis and pack everyone inside. As they sped through the streets, Mr. Rosenkranz led the older children through the *Kol Nidrei* prayer

recited at the commencement of *Yom Kippur*. They managed to
arrive and bring their various little bundles indoors just in time
to hear the cantor conclude the recital of *Kol Nidrei* with the
words "and be forgiven." Nine of the *Aseres Yemei Teshuvah*,
the Ten Days of Repentance, had passed, and *Yom Kippur*, the
Day of Atonement, had begun.

During the period the family was in Sweden, Mr. Rosenkranz
taught at the school set up in the Orthodox refugee camp at
Helsjon. After the war, they returned to Copenhagen. Some of
the children emigrated to Israel, and in 1954, their parents
joined them there. Mr. Rosenkranz survived long enough to see
a goodly number of his children, most of whom settled in Israel,
start families of their own.

During the crisis period, David had remained in Copenhagen,
as active as ever. He did not leave until after *Yom Kippur*, by
which time most of his fellow congregants had been rescued.
Eventually, he too, returned to Copenhagen, where he finished
his university studies and earned a degree in microbiology.
Together with most of the rest of his siblings, he moved to Israel,
where he became a professor of biology.

After David had left Denmark for safety in Sweden, Mr.
Bertelsen continued to direct a large rescue organization until he
was brought to the attention of the Gestapo and also fled to
Sweden, later joined by his wife who, though arrested by the
Gestapo, was later released.

Eventually earning the title of "Doctor," Bertelsen maintained warm contacts with the Jews he had met during the rescue
operation and the subsequent exile in Sweden. As a resistance
hero and a writer on religious philosophy, he continued to argue
to his fellow Danes against anti-Semitism.

COPENHAGEN, DENMARK, 1943

W hen the Ole Suhr Street rabbi had warned his congregants, the Wednesday before *Rosh Hashanah*, of the impending Gestapo raid, not all reacted by first going into hiding, as did the Rosenkranzes. Some plunged into immediate action to escape.

Benjamin Silber, one of the young men in the congregation, was absolutely stunned by the news. He had grown up all his life in Denmark, among extremely nice and friendly Gentiles. War had not ravaged the country for centuries. Even the conquest by the Germans in 1940 had been virtually bloodless; the Danes had capitulated almost immediately to vastly superior forces. Occasionally, there would be a British air attack on the shipyards which would cause some excitement, but otherwise a person living in Copenhagen hardly felt the World War raging over five continents. The idea that Jews were to be seized violently and carried off against their will was completely foreign to Benjamin. He was recently engaged, had started a business and had made numerous plans for the next few months. Suddenly, all that was to be turned upside down! He had never gone through the experience of recurrent persecution that teaches one to wait things out.

His fiancee's father searched him out in the crowd. The older man had not yet realized how thorough an operation the Gestapo was planning; he thought the Germans' goal was to collect some young people to work as slave laborers in their armaments factories.

Although he had two other boys at home, he hoped that they were young enough to be safe from the predators. But Benjamin was another story.

"Denmark is no place, right now, for people your age," he told Benjamin. "If you and your brother are planning to escape to Sweden, I would like you to take Leah and her brother Yehudah with you."

Benjamin nodded, fully agreeing to that assessment.

"We will get to work on it right away," he replied. "Have them get ready in case we can arrange to leave tonight."

After a brief consultation, Benjamin and his brother Reuven divided up the tasks. Benjamin would bike to the coast to buy a boat and hire a guide, while Reuven would get together the necessary funds. A blue-eyed blond, Benjamin passed very easily for a Dane and was not at all nervous about travelling despite the Gestapo being on the prowl. But later, at night, when he planned to take dark-haired Leah in a taxi, there would be more reason to worry. In this country of blond, blue-eyed Scandinavians, the Jews were very conspicuous.

Reaching the coast, he pulled to a stop in front of the resort where his family usually spent vacations. The proprietress recognized him and was very sympathetic when he explained what he was planning to do and why. The Danes were very civilized people and the barbaric German treatment of the Jews appalled them.

The woman's husband was a fisherman, and the couple agreed to sell their outboard motor boat to Benjamin. They also helped him find another fisherman who would be willing to risk secretly piloting Benjamin's group across the sound to the Swedish coast. After getting together the money for the boat, Benjamin was to leave the banknotes in a certain hollow tree, pick up the guide and then have his party wade out to the point where the boat was moored. Since the sea bottom sloped very gradually near the shore, they would have to wade out nearly half a mile till the water was knee-deep. At that point, where the shelf suddenly ended and the water deepened abruptly, there was a pile driven into the sea floor, to which the boat would be tied.

Well-satisfied with his morning's work, Benjamin hurried back to Copenhagen to get his party together. Reuven had enlisted another family of four, named Meyer, for their expedition, and had assembled cash amounting to more than twice what the boat would cost. That was just as well, for they needed money to live on once they reached Sweden.

According to the plan, they would take a taxi out to the coast under cover of darkness, which meant travelling after the beginning of the festival. That, more than anything else, brought home to Benjamin the fact that they were fleeing for their lives. Only under such a circumstance was it permissible to drive on *Rosh Hashanah*. They were the only group from their congregation who had made plans to leave that night for Sweden. Many of the congregants, as the Rosenkranzes of the previous episode, went underground in Denmark to see if the raid actually materialized and to watch how the situation developed.

It was the strangest *Rosh Hashanah* Benjamin had ever spent. He and his party met the Meyers and their two children in the resort's parking lot. Motioning them all into silence, Benjamin led the way to the beach. The shore area was under constant patrol by the Germans to prevent illicit traffic between Denmark and Sweden. All non-commercial boats had long since been removed from the area. Avoiding the routine patrols was a delicate enough matter, and if a big raid was in the offing, the Gestapo might be taking extra precautions to prevent people from escaping by the very route Benjamin had planned to use.

Benjamin, with the group in tow, had no difficulty finding the hollow tree despite the dark. He deposited the packet of bills his brother had prepared, and then, together with the guide who had been waiting for them at the appointed spot, the group proceeded down to the water's edge. The late September evening was already quite chilly, and as they waded into the bitterly cold water, Benjamin was glad that Leah was wearing a fur coat. The two Meyer children, aged eight and ten, marched on resolutely, though Benjamin could see that they were both shivering. The water seemed to stretch away, perfectly featureless, on all sides of them. The only reliable indication they were moving in the right direction was a very gradual deepening of the water, from ankle to shin. The numbing cold gradually crept higher and higher up their legs, until it was almost at the knees.

Suddenly, the fisherman accompanying them motioned toward something ahead. By squinting his eyes, Benjamin could just make out the dark outline of a boat, and he could now hear a faint slap of waves against its side. The fisherman scrambled deftly into the boat and helped the members of the group board one by one. The drippings of their wet clothes trickled down into the small pool of dirty water on the boat's floor. Glancing down at that ominous little pool, Benjamin was very sorry he had not thought to bring something to bail with.

The passengers distributed themselves on the board seats. With the extra weight, the boat rode noticeably lower in the water. Benjamin looked toward the shore, but the beach was practically invisible in the dark. For all he knew, it could be swarming with green uniforms.

While the two families were trying to settle themselves without unduly rocking the boat, the fisherman set to work on starting the outboard motor. Fitting the knot at the end of a string into a waiting notch, he wrapped the string several times around a wheel rim on the motor, then pulled it off with a sudden jerk. The motor turned over a couple of times, coughed and died. Undaunted, he rewrapped the string and yanked it off again with yet more force. The motor gave a louder sputter before dying again. The noise seemed very loud in the still air, and Benjamin might have glanced nervously in the direction of the beach, but he did not want to worry anyone else. The fisherman made a third unsuccessful attempt to start the motor and, when that failed, unscrewed the cap on the gas tank to see if there was enough fuel inside. Indeed, the tank had been filled to the brim, as promised. The problem was a malfunction in the motor itself.

Realizing that their escape must be delayed, the other passengers were afflicted by the same worries that plagued Benjamin. Everyone peered into the moonless night, fearing the presence of a patrol boat or a Gestapo shore patrol, the glimmer of headlights or the flash of a searchlight.

On one such survey of their surroundings, Benjamin noticed what seemed to be a patch of thick darkness off to one side of them. He signaled to the boatman, and the two of them climbed out of the boat and waded off in that direction together, with Reuven trailing along behind them. After a short walk, they came to a pile driven into the sea bottom, with an outboard motor boat, somewhat smaller than theirs, tied onto it.

As soon as Reuven caught up with them, the three men held a consultation about the ethics of the situation. Surely, they were justified in switching boats. But perhaps they should pay for the new boat, too, since if the noise of their departure was detected by a passing shore patrol, the first boat could well be confiscated. Benjamin wrote a note explaining what had happened, took from Reuven a sum of money equal to the price they had struck for the first boat, and waded ashore to deposit note and money in the hollow tree with the first bundle of banknotes. Meanwhile, the guide and Reuven oversaw the transfer of the other passengers from the original boat to the new one. The second vessel, not really intended to hold so many people, had settled dangerously low in the water by the time they were all aboard. It had, however, one overwhelming advantage over the first boat. Its motor started!

The first section of the trip was uneventful, as the purring motor carried them farther and farther from the shore and out of its guards' reach. Once they were away from the shelf, the sea bed dropped off very steeply. After an hour's travelling, they were over very deep water.

In the center section of the sound, a very swift current runs from the Baltic Sea to the North Sea. The shallow waves near the shore were replaced by deeper troughs and higher crests. Each dip down into a trough splashed a little more water into a widening pool at the passengers' feet. In order to compensate for the drift, the boat's pilot kept glancing up at the stars, trying to calculate how far off course the current was carrying them. Benjamin and the others could do nothing to help him except pray, so they set to work trying to reconstruct from memory as much of the *Rosh Hashanah* service as possible.

It was somewhere out in the deeper waters of the sound that the German patrol boat was encountered. The Meyer children had been dozing, leaning against their parents, when one of the adults on guard noticed a glimmer of light ahead of them. He alerted the fisherman, who instantly shut off the motor, and all eyes turned in the direction of the light.

"Everybody duck!" commanded Benjamin. "It's a search-light!"

All the passengers crouched down in the dirty water on the boat's floor, huddled low so that no part of their bodies would show above the vessel's side. For the moment, it was a blessing that the boat was riding so low in the water. The German vessel, riding parallel to the coast, was sweeping its menacing search-light in a wide arc in front of it, so that the cone of light just skimmed the top of the wave. Staying motionless and tense, the escapees could hear the fearful motor now, getting gradually louder, and realized that soon the critical searchlight would sweep over their precarious position. All was in the hands of Heaven. If the light swept past them while they were raised up on a crest their boat would surely be noticed by the soldiers directing the beam. If, on the other hand, it passed by them while they were down in a trough, the neighboring crest would hide them from view. Benjamin found himself tensing each time the boat was lifted upward, with only a short time to relax each time it sank downward again. Unwilling to endanger everyone by peeking over the edge, he had no notion how close the probing searchlight was.

Up . . . down. Up . . . down.

Then, while the boat was at the bottom of the troughs, Benjamin caught a glint of light from the top of the next crest and realized that the searchlight was passing overhead! By the time they began to rise again it was already past their position. The noise of the patrol boat rose to a crescendo and then began to descend again. By the time the light was turned back to their side again, they would be in the blind spot behind the patrol boat. They were safe!

When the noise of the German boat had completely faded away in the distance, the cramped passengers got up from the boat's floor and resumed their seats. Shivering in the night breeze, they sat trying to wring the bilge water out of their garments' hems, while the navigator tried to get his bearings. The stars would tell him which way was east or west, but they could not tell him how far east or west the boat was situated. How far had the current carried them while the motor had been shut off? Without knowing on which stretch of the twisting sound they were located, he did not know exactly in which direction lay the closest point on the Swedish coast. In order to choose a proper bearing, he also had to guess the speed of the current. After some hesitation, he chose a direction, started the motor and headed the boat in a generally easterly direction. The night was twelve hours long, but a good part of it was already gone, and they had to reach the safety of the opposite coast before the break of dawn.

Later in the night, there was one more alarm as a second

patrol boat passed them. Once again, they all crouched together in the deepening puddle of bilge water, for minutes which seemed like hours. Once again, they escaped detection, and once again, the pilot hesitated over the choice of a bearing. Once again, the small craft plowed eastward through the featureless waves. Benjamin glanced at his watch in disquietude. The trip, which should have taken three hours, had already stretched into six or seven. The fisherman seemed to share his concern that they must be off course. He stopped the boat, rechecked the positions of the stars and then set off again at a somewhat different angle, with Benjamin hoping it was in the right direction.

The trip was entering its eighth hour, and dawn was looming. The pool of water in the bottom of the boat was getting dangerously deep, and the boat rode lower and lower in the water with each passing hour. Benjamin doubted it could stay afloat for another sixty minutes.

Off in the east, there was a slight lightening in the sky, and they all gazed in that direction in hope of sighting land. Someone noticed a dark smudge off to one side. The passengers had to be reminded not to stand up in their excitement. The guide turned the boat in the direction of that promising dark streak. Soon, as the sky brightened a bit more, they could make out wharves along the shore, and even tiny figures standing on them. When they drew close enough to make out details, they caught their breaths in shock. The men ashore were dressed in green uniforms! Somehow they must have gotten turned around and ended up back in German-controlled territory!

The fisherman was about to turn the boat around and flee back toward the open sea, when the nearest of the men beckoned them to land and shouted something in Swedish. They scrutinized the shore again, and then Benjamin relaxed. These were Swedish soldiers, not Germans!

The little boat nosed in toward the port, and the passengers all gratefully disembarked. Though they were the first group of Jewish refugees to arrive in Sweden, the Swedish government was already prepared. The Danish government had secretly wired the Swedes a list of the names of all Jews in Denmark. Benjamin and his group were taken to the police station and asked to give their names. When the names checked out with the Danish list, that was considered adequate identification and substituted for the passports they lacked. They were fed, allowed to warm up, then taken to the nearest town with a Jewish community and released in the custody of the rabbi.

They arrived in time to hear the blowing of the *shofar* announcing the Day of Judgment and calling upon the Jews to repent.

Benjamin and Leah married after they had been in Sweden for a year. They later moved to America, where Benjamin started a business, as did his brother Reuven. When their children were settled, Benjamin and Leah emigrated to Israel, where two of Leah's brothers preside over their *yeshivos*.

One branch at the top of a tall tree is whipped by the wind and scorched by the flames. One by one, its seeds are torn off, plummeting into the fire below. The conflagration begins to subside, but then the branch does break off, tearing off the last two seeds as it falls. Quickly separated, they whirl off in a dizzy flight above the smoldering embers.

THE BARE BRANCH   4

T he war had started only two days before, and already
Tziporah Levy's family was homeless. Now, as hundreds
of other refugees from the border town of Kalisz, they were
walking, walking, walking down country lanes, with no idea
where they were headed.

The shock of being turned out of their homes had unsettled
people's judgment. One woman ahead of Tziporah was clutching a completely useless object with all her might. Another
struggled to drag along a bundle much too heavy for her.

Tziporah's father and mother, Gerer *chassidim*, decided to
head for the small town of Kozhminik, where they had cousins
with whom they hoped to find shelter. Some of the eight
children were quite young, and it would be hard for them to walk
further.

When they got to Kozhminik, they heard a commotion from
a distance behind. The refugees scattered in fright and took

117

cover. In hiding, Tziporah found herself with three friends from the Bnos Agudas Yisrael youth group to which she belonged. They peeked out and saw Polish soldiers in uniform sprinting down the road, their guns discarded and their hands held high above their heads. Close after them ran a troop of German infantrymen, guns firmly in hand.

One of the girls, Guta Grinberg, whispered, "We are witnessing history."

When the soldiers had passed, the girls shook hands in parting.

"Who knows if we will ever see each other again?" said Guta.

Indeed, they never would.

For *Rosh Hashanah*, the family moved back to Kalisz, not to their old apartment, but to one in a more Jewish section. Because of the emergency, the men did not dare pray in the Gerer *shtiebel* but in a private apartment, and the girls were placed on guard. They took their responsibility quite naturally, for Gerer *chassidim* have a distinctive approach to life, one which encourages women to nurture self-reliance and independence. The girls chose Polish names for themselves, so that they could call each other without attracting attention from the Gentiles. They each stayed posted on various street corners, in courtyards and stairwells, pretending to play or chat but actually keeping watch all the time. They had worked out signals, various shouts, cries or summons, by which to relay warnings to the praying men in time for them to scatter.

Armistice Day, November 11, had been a national holiday in Poland, celebrating the defeat of Germany in World War I and the resultant creation of an independent Poland. In revenge, the Germans chose that day to dislodge all Poles and Jews from Kalisz, replacing them with loyal ethnic Germans brought from the newly conquered territories.

The Levys moved several times during the next months, from relative to relative, looking for some way to sustain themselves. Since Mr. Levy had a full beard, he could not appear in public, and there was no way he could work. Tziporah's brothers were in danger of being hauled off to forced labor if they were seen in public. It therefore fell to the girls to find ways to support the family.

Since Jews were being squeezed out of regular employment, they had to support the family by bartering one food for another. For example, one kilo of sugar could be exchanged for ten loaves of bread, if one could get hold of the sugar. Legally, sugar was not available to Jews.

Half of the children in the Levy family were dark, and half were fair. Tziporah and her brother Mendel were among the dark ones, and they looked almost exactly like their father. The little children, acquiring wisdom beyond their age, grew into adults in a few hours. Six-year-old Sarah was one of the blondes.

"Mama," she proposed. "Wash my hair with chamomile tea so that it will be light. Braid it up very tight at night. In the morning, I'll comb it out wavy like a *shiksele* and go buy a kilo of sugar. I'll only go once a day," she added thoughtfully, "so that no one will get suspicious."

The older children were careful to speak with the little ones in Polish, so that they would have authentic-sounding accents.

Finally, in the town of Warte, the family found a place to settle and a way to survive. The apartment had only two drawbacks, but major ones. It was very small, and it was directly across the Gestapo office. Tziporah's father would sit up three-quarters of the night learning Torah, the blacked-out window ironically overlooking the very door of the Gestapo headquarters, while the others slept on pallets on the floor around him.

As for sustenance, as long as a Jew retains his commercial instinct and has a bit of freedom to exercise it, he can find a way to wrest a living from an unwelcoming world. Somewhere, someone must want something and be willing to pay money to obtain it.

The entire burden of supporting ten people fell on Tziporah's shoulders, and she became a black-marketeer. Dark hair, Jewish nose and all, she would sally out of Warte dressed like a Pole, heading for the nearby city of Zdunska-Wola.

There, she had another friend from Bnos, Leah Bresler, who was a seamstress with many Gentile clients.

"It's a shame," Leah would say, while fitting a garment, "how understocked the stores are."

"It's just terrible," her client would agree. "I've been looking all over for honey for my sore throat, and I can't find any anywhere."

"If you could just turn around a bit—there, that's right. You know, I have a friend, a refugee from Kalisz, who could do the running around for you. I bet she could ferret out a jar of honey from somewhere."

"You think so?" the client would ask. "I'd be willing to pay a good price for her trouble."

"I expect to see her tomorrow," Leah would say. "I'll ask her to get it for you. Only, you know how difficult the situation of those refugees is. You'll have to advance a few *zlotys* so that she can pay for the goods."

Leah would then give Tziporah the money and the list of goods the women wanted, and Tziporah would go to her black market contacts. Supply was very irregular, and she could not always find what she was sent for. Contraband goods often changed hands several times, each person taking a cut. Still, by diligence and persistence, she managed to turn enough of a profit to keep bread on her family's table.

A kind family allowed her to sleep on their floor while she was working. One week, she did not manage to get out of the city until Friday afternoon. She had bad luck finding a Gentile wagoner going her direction, and by late afternoon she was still far from home. Despairing of reaching home by *Shabbos*, she got off the wagon when it passed through the town of Sheretz, which she knew to have a Jewish community, and arrived at the Jewish section just at dusk.

She did not actually know anyone in the town, and of course, no one had prepared for her. Nonetheless, they made her feel welcome, sharing their meager ration of bread and the hot liquid that passed for coffee and making up a pallet for her on the same floor where many other people were ready to bed down. It was true Jewish hospitality.

LODZ, POLAND • 1942

On a hot day in the summer of 1942, all the Jews of Warte were ordered to assemble in a large open space. They were marched in family groups past one of the SS men, who divided them into two groups. There was no discernible logic about the selections. Tziporah and her three oldest brothers were sent to one side, their parents and their younger siblings to another. Tziporah and her three brothers were loaded onto trucks with the other young people.

Already in shock from seeing their parents and sisters forcibly led away, they clung together with desperate determination. Their truck contained about forty men and twenty women. The convoy of trucks, loaded with Jews, drove down the main highway toward the nearest railroad station, twelve kilometers from Warte.

The driver cut a corner very sharply, and there was a sudden lurch as one of the truck's wheels slipped into a pothole. The entire truck quivered, tilted and flipped over onto its roof into a ditch along the side of the road, throwing all the passengers from their seats.

Tziporah felt a shooting pain in her hand, which took the force of the fall. Pandemonium broke loose as the passengers were hauled out through the back of the truck. Trying to ignore the pain in her hand, Tziporah called out desperately for her brothers over the din of shouts and screams.

Once outside and on her feet, she was able to look around. The driver had been killed, but most of the passengers had survived, including, to her relief, all three of her brothers. One suffered a broken hand, as did she, but at least they could all walk. That was crucial, for their captors decided to have them march the rest of the way to the train depot.

Tziporah was trying to put up a brave front and not let the SS guards see her hand was hurt, afraid they would simply shoot anyone they judged unfit for work. The town butcher, Mr. Meyerowicz, thought Tziporah's thumb was simply dislocated.

"Here," he said, taking her hand and starting to twist it. "I'll put that back in place for you."

Tziporah, in agonizing pain, bit hard on her lip to avoid screaming.

"Stop!" someone protested. "Don't you see that she is turning blue?"

They were marched into the station at double time. No passenger train was waiting there. Instead, there was a long row of boxcars, some of them padlocked. Trucks were standing by the station, emptied of the Jews whose shouts and protests issued from the locked boxcars.

"*Juden! Herein!*" shouted the guards, urging them forward, with painful blows, to one box-car that still had standing room. They scrambled quickly aboard, the door was slammed shut, and a padlock was snapped in place.

It was the middle of a hot day in August, the intense heat was unbearable, and in the closed box-car packed tight with standing people, there was hardly any air to breathe. Even when the train began lurching forward, not a breath of fresh air managed to force its way in to relieve the stifling heat. Shockingly, neither were there any sanitary arrangements made, nor was any drinking water provided. When the train pulled into a station, the suffering victims called out to a guard for water.

"It's so hot in here!" they protested. "We are all dying of thirst!"

He sneered at them and laughed with scorn. "I see you're not hot. You haven't taken off your clothes!"

Tziporah looked at him with contempt. As if mere heat would be a reason for immodesty!

When, many hours later, the train halted and the padlocks were removed, everyone in the car was ravenous, thirsty and weak. Someone said they were in Lodz. Tziporah felt a stir of hope. She had an uncle in the Lodz ghetto. Maybe he could help.

The new arrivals were packed into the central prison, penned in by a chain-link fence. On the other side of the fence were women from the ghetto proper, dressed in tattered clothing and looking emaciated. As the Jews from the trains walked through the corridor toward their destination, they were each handed a quarter loaf of bread. The ghetto women began holding out their hands and begging. "Bread! Bread! Give it to me!"

Tziporah felt deeply offended at the time. Those women must know by now what conditions were on the transports. How could they beg bread from people who had had neither food nor water for so long? It was not only a chilling warning of the food shortages in the ghetto, it also seemed that starvation was reducing the ghetto residents to an animal level.

Her glance sped over the ghetto residents across the fence and halted as she recognized two of her cousins. She went over to the fence and they gave her their address. Her uncle had heard of the transports coming in from their area and had sent his children to find any friends or relatives who might be among the new arrivals.

From the prison, they were taken to a bathhouse, where they washed and their clothes were fumigated. As they came out, Tziporah encountered another friend from her Bnos days, Faiga Zelicka, who gave Tziporah her family's address and urged her to come visit. "We'll give you some laundry and bed-clothes."

Tziporah was deeply ashamed at this suggestion of charity. They had arrived with no clothing or personal belongings. Her long braids had come unpinned and hung down disheveled from the accident in the truck. She was very conscious of arousing pity and resolved not to accept handouts from Faiga.

Tziporah and her brothers managed to stay together while released into the residential part of the confining ghetto. They reported to the ghetto housing office and were assigned one room at the very edge of the ghetto, on a street divided by a fence separating them from the "Aryan" section. It was an abandoned apartment, without door or windows. The winters had been hard, and the local residents had burned the wood for fuel. The wooden floor had once contained a trap door, covering the entrance to the cellar normally used for food storage. It had recently served as a bomb shelter and was littered with shards of glass from broken utensils. The trap door was now gone, and an unwary walker could fall into the cellar.

They were issued iron beds, for which they made straw mattresses. They also received a small, low stove such as peasants used in the summer. The fuel was sawdust, and since there was no exhaust for the smoke, it filled the room with soot and smoke. Tziporah, spirited as ever, stood with her hands on her hips and proclaimed, "On this I am supposed to cook? I am expected to prepare meals on this thing?"

Tziporah and her brothers collected their bread rations, one kilogram loaf per person every eight days. Not having a cabinet in their room, they used the window sill for storage. Others who had already been in Lodz for a day or two called out to them.

"You are making a mistake," they asserted. "You must divide up the rations among yourselves so that none of you will take more than their share."

The Levy children did not listen. Throughout their years in Lodz, they had kept all their supplies together. In one way, however, this was a mistake, not because they short-changed each other, but because each one tried to cut his own ration short, for the others' sake.

They paid their uncle a visit. Compared to their own bare dwelling, the house was chock-full of objects, among them a pair of scissors. The aunt cut off Tziporah's long-treasured braids for her. Much though it hurt Tziporah to part with them, it was hardly practical to have long hair under the current circumstances.

Tziporah described their journey to the house, ending with how the women wanted their bread.

"What nerve!" Tziporah exclaimed.

"When you know all the facts, Tziporah," said Uncle Yaakov sadly, "you'll judge them more charitably. You see, most of the people passing down that corridor have been on the way to their deaths. It was hard for those starving women to see all that bread go to waste. Food is very scarce."

From her uncle's description of the situation in the ghetto, Tziporah now understood that life in Warte had been better. In the small towns, there was still some minimal contact with the population, some way to fight. Ghetto Lodz was hermetically sealed, lacking any contact at all with the people outside the walls who were, in any case, ethnic Germans implacably hostile to the Jews. Here they would have to get ghetto jobs and submit to the conditions dictated to them by the authorities, or they would not obtain even minimal sustenance. The situation was thoroughly distressing.

Tziporah and her brother Yaakov proceeded to a clinic, where they finally had their hands put in casts. The nurse took pity on Tziporah, who was obviously still in great pain.

"I'll tell you what," she offered. "I'm going to arrange for you to stay here until that hand heals a bit."

"I don't want to stay," refused Tziporah. Her instinct still told her it was not wise to be singled out as being weak or injured.

"Listen," said the nurse. "You are new, so you don't understand what a favor I am doing you. The food in the hospital is better than that outside. You won't have to work for it."

"I'll manage," said Tziporah. "I don't want to be separated from my brothers."

"Don't be silly," laughed another of the staff members. "Your brothers would agree. You don't know what means people resort to in order to get their relatives in here. Tears, pleading, bribes, influence."

Tziporah continued to insist on leaving. As she walked out, they were still laughing at her.

But Tziporah's firm refusal to stay worked in her favor. The next night, the Germans made a lightning raid and cleared out all the hospitals, sending the invalids to an unknown destination. All of Lodz went into shock, for almost everyone had some relative or friend in one of the hospitals. Indeed, as the nurses said, many had struggled, pleaded and bribed to get their loved ones admitted, but now everything was turned upside down. They had expended all that effort for what had turned out to be a death warrant. The guilt exacerbated their mourning. Tziporah could only be thankful that by some miracle she had stood firm under the pressure and refused to remain in the hospital.

A few days later, on September 5, the Germans declared a general, daytime curfew. The Jewish police went from house to house taking away the children, the old people, the sick and the injured. The families and children of the Jewish policemen had been put in a safe place, as hostages to ensure their wholehearted cooperation. Feather beds were ruthlessly ripped open or bayonetted in case there was a child sewn up inside, as there often was. A mother whose child was being taken tied a ribbon in the little girl's hair, in the hope that she might be saved from danger by some German who would take a liking to her. Whole cartloads of children were rushed through the streets, with cries of "Mama, Mama!" emanating from them.

Within its first hours, the *Aktion* reached the apartment where Tziporah and her brothers were staying. They agreed quickly that all who might escape from wherever they were being taken were to return to the apartment as soon as possible. The police brought Tziporah to a large public building. Through the open door, she could see that coffee and bread were being dispensed to the people waiting there.

"This looks too much like taking up permanent residence," she thought, and she decided that she had to find some way out.

Fortunately, pandemonium was still reigning and her captors were highly disorganized. She hung back as others pushed through the door, and she succeeded in slipping into an alleyway alongside the building. It was already dusk. Behind the building was a wide lawn, and in the back of the yard, a wall about one story high. The only person in sight was a man standing on the lawn, engaged in tossing a child to safety over the wall. There was no exit from the yard.

Tziporah hurried up to the man. "Perhaps you could throw me over, too?" she requested.

"I can try," agreed the man. Tziporah climbed up on his shoulders. He grasped her by the ankles and heaved her. She tumbled down the other side onto a thick stand of tall grass, which broke most of the fall's force.

Tziporah lay still in the grass, wondering if she were outside the ghetto. If so, she would be in trouble, for any Pole or German who found her might shoot her on the spot. The evening dew had fallen, and she rubbed her face in the damp grass in the hope that it would revive her and help her think more clearly. Off in the distance, she saw a glimmer of light, and she began to drag herself slowly in its direction, remaining entirely flat on the ground and hidden by the tall grass. As she moved, she became conscious of other similar clandestine movements to her right and left, indicating that she was not the only person hiding out in this field.

As she neared the light, which was held by some person, she heard a faint conversation between the person holding the light and someone else. Finally, she caught the intonation of Yiddish, and she felt much relieved. This meant she was still inside the ghetto.

A form loomed up in front of her, and she recognized the characteristic movements of her brother Mendel. How wonderful to find him here, out of all the tens of thousands of people in the ghetto. She signalled to him, and he approached her. They were much relieved to see they had both escaped from almost certain consignment to a transport. He was dripping and smelly, having escaped through the sewage pipes. Together they cautiously edged their way home. There, they found their remaining brothers safe as well. Yaakov had also escaped through the sewage system, aided by Lodz boys who knew all the twists and turns. Leibush had gotten away by hopping onto a cart hauling corpses and helping the crew with their loading.

When an eight-day-long curfew, the *Sperre*, was finally lifted, the ghetto inhabitants were weak from hunger and bruised in spirit. Their children, the future of the Jewish people, had been torn from them. No one had been left but the workers.

Until the previous autumn, the children of the ghetto had gone to ghetto schools, which had also given them some sort of a hot meal for lunch. They had known that they were missing a great deal of what most children take for granted. Outside the walls there was a park with a carousel. The ghetto children would hover around that part of the fence to hear snatches of gay lilting music or catch a flash of swirling color through a crack. One of Tziporah's acquaintances had been a kindergarten teacher. On their "nature walks," she could point out a chicken through a crack in the fence, or at least let the children hear a rooster crow from the "Aryan side." However, in trying to describe an egg to children who had never seen such a thing, she found her task hopeless. Now they had been carried off. They would never know any of the joys of childhood.

In a physical sense, the lot of the ghetto improved slightly after the mass deportation. The ghetto was no longer so overcrowded. Although the food rations were decreased accordingly, there was still a little more to go around, a few more potato cubes in the soup dished out in the workshops.

The Levys applied to the ghetto labor office for work assignments. Tziporah pulled her sleeve down so it would cover her cast. Mendel, Leibush and Tziporah were placed in the "resorts," the huge workshops engaged in war production. Mendel's resort was a factory for cigarettes. Leibush got an assignment cleaning the streets. Yaakov did not work in a resort. Every family tried to keep one member working elsewhere, who would be free from the resort's twelve-hour shifts, so that he might pick up extra ration allotments, light the fire in the evening and run other errands. Tziporah's resort was a huge hall containing fifteen tables, with four or five women on each side. They were all engaged in separating blocks of insulating material into thin sheets with specially designed tools. There was a break in the middle of the day, when they went down to the courtyard and lined up holding beaten tin pots for a portion of watery soup. Tziporah's pot, like those of her brothers, had been rescued from a refuse pile. Was the previous owner Jewish? Was it a milk pot or a meat pot? Tragically, all these questions had become irrelevant in the life-and-death circumstances.

Tziporah noticed and recognized one of the other workers following her with her eyes, a tall girl who had a distinctive appearance. She was Minia Slenska, one of the activists in Bnos, and was probably trying to decide whether or not she recognized Tziporah. But Tziporah did not want to be recognized. She was too ashamed of how far she had come down in the world.

After a few weeks, Tziporah and her brothers managed to save up a treasure, an entire half loaf of bread. With this, they bought themselves the right to a different apartment, one with doors and windows, farther from the ghetto wall.

When they got their rations, they performed a little ritual. They would mix together a little sugar, a little fat and a few oats, and call it halvah. Each one would get a small spoonful.

A few children had survived the long, starving curfew and eventually came out of their hiding-places. There were no schools, so they played, begged or sold items of ghetto manufacture. One of these items was a long-lasting toffee manufactured out of something normally considered inedible. "Hard as a rock!" the children would praise their wares, since a candy which did not melt away was much more satisfying. "Like a brick! Like an entire house!" The reappearance of children on the streets was a sign of the eternity of the Jewish people.

Tziporah's brothers found *tefillin* for themselves among the piles of discards. On the whole, praying had to be done at home. Everything was difficult; hunger and illness sapped their energy.

Community life continued in the evenings after work.

Movement inside the ghetto was relatively free, as long as one stayed away from the streets bordering the "Aryan" side. The girls in Tziporah's circle tried to compensate for the bitter ghetto life by helping each other wherever possible. Those who had a few possessions tried to share them with others who, as the Levy family, arrived without personal possessions or even a blanket to keep out the cold at night. Since these offers always entailed personal sacrifice, Tziporah turned them down.

Occasionally, Tziporah went to classes given by teachers from Beis Yaakov who were personal students of Sarah Schenirer. The teachers and the girls struggled, by studying *Tanach*, to find some comfort in their trials. They delved into the past, better to understand the present and to believe in a future. Faiga Zelicka was one of the teachers, but Tziporah was still avoiding her. At one such class Tziporah ran into Minia, who finally succeeded in recognizing her.

"You *are* Tziporah Levy. Why have you been avoiding me?"

Tziporah looked down, embarrassed, and did not know how to answer.

"We heard that Tziporah Levy had arrived in Lodz, and we were trying to find out what resort you were working in."

It was probably Faiga who had told them. Tziporah submitted to a scolding and gave up her attempts to hide her presence in Lodz. She even went to look for Faiga, but it was too late. Her father had passed away, and she no longer lived at the address she had given.

In Tziporah's resort, the girls from Bnos, among them Minia Basya Weisgold and Rachel Greenbaum, tried to organize a way to avoid personally desecrating *Shabbos*. The leaders of the group remained strong and firm in the worst of situations. They tried to arrange for only one member of their group to be at each table. Minia enlisted the noninterference of the manager, a Mr.

Rosenberg. Each table had a joint daily quota, a situation which led to many arguments and accusations of slacking, and if they achieved more than the minimum, they were eligible for certain privileges, which created fierce competition among different tables. The Germans loved to create that kind of bickering among the Jews.

Any girl who desired to avoid working *Shabbos* would have to convince the other women at her table to compensate by producing more, in return for a promise to work extra hard on the remaining days of the week. Since the other women were also Jewish, this did not decrease the total amount of *Shabbos* desecration, but it was surely beneficial for the morale of the religious Jews.

It goes without saying that on *Shabbos*, they had to sit in their normal places for the full twelve hours, their work materials in front of them. If an inspector would come to tour the resort, each of the girl's neighbors would push a few finished sheets discreetly in her direction, so that it would appear she had been producing just as much as the rest of them.

At Tziporah's table, there was another of the Bnos girls, Machcia Biawek from Lask, so their co-workers had to agree to carry a double burden. Some respected the girls for wanting to refrain from work, some took a "let them do what they want" attitude, and some were opposed. "After all we have been through, who wants to keep *Shabbos*?"

Tziporah could understand how the women in the latter group had become so spiritually crushed to have abandoned observance. She considered it amazing that there were any who held up.

At home, the Levy children made every possible effort to leave one bread whole, for the Friday night *Shabbos* meal. This was often quite difficult, for the distribution of the bread ration was deliberately conducted once in eight days, to make it come out on a different day of the week each time. If the bread was distributed on Saturday, it was hard to have a full loaf left a week later. Next to the loaf, they would place a spoonful of food, to substitute for the second loaf normally placed on a *Shabbos* table. In the ghetto, life was a battle for everyone. Still, each person, each family, could raise the level of that battle. It made a great difference whether one was battling for bare subsistence or struggling to keep a loaf of bread whole for *Shabbos*.

Just before Passover, Leibush weakened and took ill. He had always been what was known as a "silken young man," quiet, refined and gentle. He called his sister and brothers to his bedside.

"I am passing from the world for want of a piece of bread," he told them. "As for you, quick, take my ration-book and get my rations before I die. I know that the fat in the bread comes from pork. It is no longer for me. You have it."

A few hours later, he was gone.

Tziporah and her other two brothers hung on and stayed together for another year and a half, until the ghetto was liquidated. There were periods when the rations did not arrive, and everyone was starving. There were periods when vitamin deficiencies sapped all their strength. Always, they were hungry.

BERGEN-BELSEN, GERMANY • 1944-1945

I n 1944, Mendel was taken on a transport. With the liquidation of the ghetto, the surviving remnant of Tziporah's family was finally torn from her, and she was left on her own.

Biebow, the German administrator of the ghetto, declared the passengers were being transferred to a labor camp, but in fact, they were sent, without water, to Auschwitz.

From the moment the train stopped at the siding in the Birkenau section of Auschwitz, normal existence was temporarily suspended. The Jews were greeted with blows and curses, the men and women were separated and all were forced to move from place to place at a run. Tziporah, totally parted from her family, was quickly reduced to the mental state of a hunted and suffering animal. Thinking ceased. One acted by instinct.

It was instinct, an instinct of self-preservation, that told Tziporah to try to look well when passing through the *Selektzia*. She did not even know from what she had been saved, when the next shock hit. With her fellow survivors, she was driven into a room in which their hair was all shaved off.

In the heat of July, she had somehow contracted a head cold, and it was part of the crescendo of misery crashing around her that there was no rag or scrap of paper with which she could blow her nose. Yet, the instinct continued to tell her she must at all costs hide the fact that she had a cold, particularly during the selections through which they passed several times a day. The constant surreptitious sniffling gave her sinus headaches which never left her from then on.

Five women were assigned to a wooden bed the size of a dining room table. If one woman wanted to move, all five had to move in concert. A zoo would have been a cultured and refined environment by comparison.

At one point during the ordeal, Tziporah met an acquaintance, Yehudis Hirschberg, who worked in the lazarette and was able to slip her a piece of bread. The bread was badly needed, but she found it yet more soothing to be recognized and to have her existence as a person acknowledged.

The six-day period Tziporah spent in Birkenau, the women's section of Auschwitz, was an unworldly experience. Whatever the misery of slow starvation in Lodz and the shocks of the occasional *Aktionen* there, it had not been the swimming in cruelty, the drowning in cruelty that characterized Birkenau. There was no thinking, no reflection, only a quivering, shrinking, animal existence.

From Auschwitz, she was taken to a camp which supplied laborers to a large weapons factory. The Jews worked two twelve-hour shifts, one week of day shifts and one week of night shifts. Of the original two hundred and fifty prisoners brought from Auschwitz, eight were chosen for kitchen work, and the remaining prisoners were sent to the factory. Those eight girls who worked in the kitchen were the first to grow enough hair to make a part; somehow, in the kitchen, there is always some way to get a little extra to eat.

There were thousands of workers in the factory, consisting of the two hundred and fifty Jewish girls from Lodz plus large numbers of Gentile workers from other countries. Each nationality had a different food ration, depending on what extent, in the Germans' eyes, it was necessary to cultivate good relations. The Swiss, whose country was neutral, got the best food. Unlike all the other workers, the Jews were not fed at all in the factory, but only in the camp after hours. When they arrived in the morning, each of the Jewish girls was given two cards, entitling her to go out to the latrines twice during the twelve-hour shift. Only the Jewish workers were under constant guard.

Many of the Gentile workers felt sorry for the Jews, but those who actually put their sympathy to work were the Italians. They had a sunny outlook on the world, not worrying much about the future or about possible punishment for their actions. They bribed guards to get a little extra food for the Jews, they wheedled the gate guard to get extra tickets so that the girls could go out and rest, and they sent warnings when the supervisor was coming out to see why they had been gone so long.

In the evenings, the prisoners had the time for thought they had been missing in Auschwitz, and their reflections were bitter, indeed. They now began to realize that when their families had been separated from them two years earlier, it was probably to go to some place like Auschwitz. One by one, they began to face the possibility that each of them was the sole surviving member of her family.

The camp had a punishment compound for workers caught at one infraction or another, stealing or arguing or talking back. Once consigned to the punishment compound, one did not get out again. One day, Tziporah was also sent there. What was her crime? There was not enough work for the machine she operated.

By the end of three months, the number of women in the lock-up had risen to fifty. When they were not released and sent back to work, they grew convinced that they were destined for the furnaces of Auschwitz. The fact that they were barely fed lent credence to this idea; the Germans did not like to waste food on people who were going to die soon anyway. When it was announced that the prisoners were to be shipped out, one of Tziporah's friends, Leah Berliner, stinted on her own meager bread ration and risked being imprisoned herself, in order to slip Tziporah food for the journey.

The fifty Lodz evacuees from the punishment compound were once again locked in boxcars for another grueling, waterless transport. When they were let out, however, it was not the gigantic complex at Auschwitz before them, but a small station, from which they were taken to another labor camp. When they entered the gates of the camp, the women from Lodz all gave one united cry of protest and pain as they saw the other inmates, "They still have their hair!" Of all the dehumanizing treatment to which they had been subjected, the shaving of their hair struck the deepest at their self-esteem.

The new arrivals were lined up in rows as in a slave market, and the different bosses came to choose workers. The first, who obviously had "pull," was a strutting Czech. He walked up and down the line, choosing his "wares" with an arrogant motion of his hand. Tziporah was among them. He led them off to a section of a factory containing a number of machines. Then, he took an equal number of girls from his own workers, paired them with the new arrivals and sent each pair off to a different machine to explain how it worked.

Tziporah's mate had come to this camp straight from her home in 1942, without passing through Auschwitz. She not only had all her hair, she was still wearing her school uniform, with its black apron.

"You must be intelligent," her companion said, while demonstrating the operation of the machine, "if the *panichki*, the little gentleman, picked you out. Where are you from?"

"From Kalisz," answered Tziporah. "And you?"

The girl named a town on the other side of Poland.

"Oh, I know someone from there," said Tziporah. "We were together before the war in a course for Bnos counselors." She gave the name.

With that, Tziporah was established as someone who could be trusted. After ascertaining no one was listening, she whispered to Tziporah, "Did you know that it is *Chanukah*?"

"No," said Tziporah. "I've completely lost track of the Jewish calendar." Tziporah was hard-pressed just keeping track of which day was *Shabbos*. To remember which months had twenty-nine days and which had thirty, to know whether the Jewish month of *Kislev* had an extra day that year, was all beyond her.

"One of the girls who works in the kitchen is going to try to steal a little oil," she told Tziporah. "Pull a few threads out of your blanket and be ready tonight when I come for you."

Tziporah, weak and tired, lay in bed, trying not to fall asleep. When all the others in the barracks were asleep, she felt a light touch. Tziporah, clutching the threads, climbed noiselessly out of the bunk, and the two girls slipped out into the dark. The other members of the *Chanukah* conspiracy were gathered in a corner of the barrack. The threads Tziporah and others had brought were twisted into wicks and soaked in the oil.

One of the girls whispered the blessing, "Blessed are You, O G-d, our Lord, Who has sanctified us with His commandments and commanded us to light the *Chanukah* lights.

". . . Who did miracles for our fathers, in those days, in this season.

". . . Who kept us alive, sustained us and allowed us to reach this time."

The girls in the new camp still dreamed of a day at the end of the war when they would be reunited with their families. People wanted to believe things would work out well, and there was a sort of mental lassitude which hindered them from waking up from a pleasant dream. Yet gradually, the bitterness of the women from Lodz and the descriptions of Auschwitz began to affect them. Some had already had their fathers taken away while they were still home. Now they, too, began to realize their mothers and sisters and little brothers were not waiting peacefully at home for their return.

As the Russians approached their camp, the inmates were transferred to Bergen-Belsen, where Tziporah contracted typhus. She was so ill over *Pesach*, she could honestly deny having eaten any leavened food for the entire eight days.

In Bergen-Belsen, Tziporah saw, firsthand, those who were once the highest fall the lowest. Among the new arrivals in the camp were some German Jewish women, coming straight from their homes and still wearing their fur coats. The transition to camp life was so abrupt and shocking to them, they lost all control and all will to live. Even the ordinary efforts at sanitation and cleanliness, routine among the other prisoners, were soon beyond these women, who disintegrated completely.

In Bergen-Belsen, Tziporah began to feel that perhaps she had finally reached the end. For six years, her life had been an ever-narrowing tunnel. Her old world before the war had included contacts with friends and relations from all over Poland. During the years in Warte, they were much more circumscribed, but the immediate family was still together, and they knew the events taking place a few towns away. In Lodz, with only a part of her family, she was sealed in by walls. Then, as she passed through Auschwitz, she was stripped of family, of privacy, of everything but herself, alone. Now, after the typhus and the grinding hunger of Bergen-Belsen, she was no more than a walking skeleton, and she felt that even control over her body was being taken from her.

But it was not despair. The Germans had wanted to drive them to despair, to suicide. Their tormentors could not understand why they still wanted to live. But they did want to live. Their captors had not destroyed their faith in life, their conviction that if they could only hold on, this would pass and better times would come.

Tziporah was plodding along a road inside the camp with her friend Rishka Weskowicz when she finally felt that she was no longer able to carry on, to put one foot in front of the other.

"Look at this ditch," said Tziporah. "Such a fine ditch! I'm going to lie down in this ditch and stay there. If you make it through, you can tell them all that I died in the finest of ditches."

"You are not going to die," said her friend firmly. "I'm not going to let you."

"Please," said Tziporah. "Just go on and leave me alone."

"No, I won't let you stay here. You are getting to the barracks if I have to haul you there."

Indeed, Rishka nearly had to drag Tziporah to get to their quarters. Just when they arrived, a new group of prisoners came to the camp, who put heart in all of them. They were Gentile Polish girls who had been in the Warsaw underground, had been caught and had been sent to Bergen-Belsen as a punishment. But since the underground had radios, they knew about the Allied advances and the position of the front. They knew that liberation might be just days away. Even the old-time prisoners could feel that the watch over them was getting looser.

One morning, some jeeps drove in through the camp gates. The Polish girls pointed to the five-pointed stars on the hoods of the jeeps and shouted, "Those are the Americans! We are free!"

Utter pandemonium broke out. The prisoners ran and broke into the food stores. The first thing they discovered were hundreds of loaves of bread which turned out to be poisoned. The guards had prepared them for the inmates, to kill them all. However, the Allied advance had been too swift and the guards had fled without distributing the bread.

The next discovery made by the mob of prisoners was a pit filled with suitcases, each packed with watches, presumably looted by the SS from incoming prisoners. The mob, reinforced by some Russians, pressed in around the cache of watches and began snatching. With such a watch, one could buy a bit of butter. Tziporah would also have liked to take one, but she hung back, fearing that she would be trampled or smothered in that mad rush.

The Americans and British, thunderstruck at the sight of the haggard skeletons walking around in the camp, tried to rush in medical aid and supplies, but the bombed-out roads and general confusion of war made it frustratingly difficult to supply the material and staff fast enough.

The first step the Allies took was to delouse the prisoners with a poisonous powder pumped mechanically from a spray contraption looking like a miniature rocket. The lice, which had been making all the inmates so miserable and spread typhus, vanished with one treatment. Most of the prisoners had diarrhea, apparently connected with dehydration, so the medical staff set out vats of water on tables in a field and forced the prisoners to drink and drink and drink.

Then they fed them. Tragically, in this, the doctors made a serious error, which for many of the inmates proved irrevocable. The food might just as well have been poisoned, for thousands of prisoners who had been managing on the prison diet died in agony that first night, their cramped and shrunken stomachs unable to deal with the rich fare they were offered. Tziporah, like others who ate only in moderation, pulled through that night.

When the supply of hypodermic needles was exhausted, the doctors resorted to distributing packets containing three ampules of medicine to each prisoner, with instructions to bite them open and drink the contents. The nurse in charge gave Tziporah six. Her companion protested.

"I wasted so many of these on people I don't think can possibly survive," said the first nurse. "When I finally see someone who has a real chance, I want to give enough to really help."

They were moved into barracks that had been quarters for soldiers, and began to feel somewhat human again. Rabbis came from England to bring prayerbooks, *tefillin* and other religious supplies, and a kosher kitchen was organized.

Within days, lists of prisoners were circulated from camp to camp to help people locate lost relatives. When a "Mendel Levy" showed up on the list from the camp at Feldefing, Tziporah was cautious; many people had been disappointed. How many "Mendel Levys" had there been in Kalisz before the war? However, when someone arrived from Feldefing she inquired.

Indeed, he knew this Mendel Levy and had worked with him in a cigarette factory in Lodz. When he said that Mendel was always the one waking him up to join a *minyan* earlier than he wanted, Tziporah was convinced this was indeed her brother. She prepared to join a group travelling in the direction of Feldefing.

Travel for the liberated prisoners was still very difficult. A journey which should have taken them a day and a half stretched to ten days. Part of the journey was made by train, with the people clinging to the ladders on the outsides of the oil tank cars. Throughout the night, they called to each other to make sure no one had fallen off.

When she got near Feldefing, Tziporah met someone from the camp and inquired after Mendel Levy. The man laughed at her.

"You made all this trip for nothing," he told her. "Mendel Levy left for the Land of Israel a week ago."

Disheartened she continued on into Feldefing to rest and recover before going back to Bergen-Belsen. In the camp, she met a woman who had known her brother.

"He said he had a sister who might make it through," the woman said. "He was going on to the Land of Israel while he had a chance, but he hoped you would join him there. He said he would buy you a watch as a welcoming present." That already made Tziporah feel better.

When she arrived back at her own camp, exhausted from the long journey, she discovered that her friends were all packed up and ready to move out in the morning. They were undergoing training as agricultural workers, in the hope of making it easier to get Palestine certificates. Without hesitating, tired as she was, Tziporah gathered up her own things and prepared to join them. She, too, intended to get to the Land of Israel and start a new life there.

SALZHEIM, GERMANY

T he Jews had retrieved an agricultural preserve in Ceringshoff, which had served the Zionists before the war as a training ground for agricultural workers. It was now revived under the name of "Unity Kibbutz." Unity was surely the thing it lacked most, the people involved being thrown together from every possible background and political affiliation. The food was thoroughly non-kosher, so Tziporah and her friends had to cook for themselves outdoors over a wood fire. They could not get kosher meat and ate only dairy food.

As *Rosh Hashanah* approached, one of the men, Yaakov Trauber, set off for Bergen-Belsen in an attempt to obtain a *shofar* and holiday prayerbooks. As the holiday neared and the messenger still had not returned, the non-religious members of the *kibbutz* started making fun of the religious ones. As the sun was setting, Tziporah and her friends walked out to the edge of the settlement and looked off in the direction from which they hoped Yaakov would come. In the distance, they saw a wagon approaching. Just as the sun went down, someone descended the wagon and started walking along the road, carrying a bundle. It was their companion. He had brought the *shofar* and the prayerbooks. The other members of the *kibbutz* might have laughed, but in the morning, they too came to services to hear the *shofar* blown.

The religious group went to the Joint and to Agudas Yisrael and asked to be allowed to set up an agricultural settlement of their own. The request was eventually granted, and they set themselves up, five men and three women, to till the land and learn to farm in Salzheim, a suburb of Frankfurt-on-Main. A similar group joined them from a settlement at Gersfeld, and reinforcements came from Bergen-Belsen. Eventually, others joined them, until their group had grown to nearly seventy people. The *kibbutz* became the family Tziporah had lost.

The facility they had been given had been a roadside inn. It consisted of fields and barns and a building on each side of the road. One building had been the tavern, complete with a bar, a piano and a small stage. That became their dining room. There was a large kitchen in back and a large hall in front. They seated the men on one side, the women on the other. The other building had several apartments on each floor. They assigned one floor to women, one to men.

Some of the girls were from rural towns in Hungary. They knew very much about farming, such as the agricultural cycle, how to milk cows and so forth. But the two groups, the Polish and the Hungarian, never completely merged. The urbanized Polish girls, who knew how to write in Hebrew and Yiddish, considered themselves more sophisticated, better managers and, perhaps, better housekeepers. The Hungarian girls, who had been in the midst of the crisis for only one year instead of six, considered themselves more religious, better cooks and, perhaps, better housekeepers. The girls in either group took it hard if a Jew from their own country married a girl from the other; they tended to feel that in time he would come to regret his mistake.

One *Shabbos*, a group came from Bergen-Belsen to visit their facility in Salzheim. The Bergen-Belsen group felt that there should be a more stringent separation of men and women, perhaps a divider in the dining room. The Salzheim group felt that they were not ready for that. The argument raged until three o'clock in the morning, with furious voices raised on either side. Finally, they were all so hungry that they went into the kitchen and doled out the stew left heating on the stove for the next day's lunch, finishing it all off.

One function the *kibbutz* members fulfilled for each other was matchmaking. Tziporah had a friend, Yaffa Silberberg, who was vociferous in her complaints about one of the workers in the barn, Chaim Tzizovsky, whom she considered the laziest man alive, throwing all the work on the girls. Chaim took her complaints in silence. One evening at eleven, he approached Tziporah and her friend Malka with a request. He was leaving the next morning for Italy, on his way to the Land of Israel. Ever since he was a little boy, his family had intended him to marry a certain cousin who was now in Palestine. If he arrived alone, his aunt there would make the match, and he did not want it. He wanted Tziporah and Malka to persuade Yaffa to agree to marry him.

The girls went to Yaffa and then back to Chaim with her refusal. They ran back and forth between the two all night, until finally, at five in the morning, they all drank a toast to the engagement. Yaffa took her bundles and joined her fiance and the others on the truck to Italy.

One week, Tziporah had a guest for *Shabbos*, someone she had known before the war. At Friday lunch, someone was visiting one of the Salzheim men, and he seemed familiar to Tziporah. She asked her friend, but was told it was her imagination. They all had the disease of thinking people they saw looked familiar, and usually, there was nothing to it. Later, she noticed this stranger motioning to her. Is she going to pay attention to a summons from a strange man? She ignored it. He was so persistent, however, that finally she went over.

"*Shalom*, daughter of Yoel Levy!" he said. He was Leib Borenstein, one of the young Gerer *chassidim* from Kalisz, her hometown, and was in fact a relative of Tziporah's guest. He had recognized Tziporah by her resemblance to her father and brother.

Friday night, Tziporah noticed that Leib was staying for *Shabbos*. The next morning David Kristal, his host, approached her. He and Leib had been together in the camps. He described how close they had been and the efforts they had expended to review their studies. His friend had asked him to speak to Tziporah. Having seen that there was a daughter of Yoel Levy at Salzheim, he did not want to leave until Tziporah would agree to be his wife.

The engagement and wedding were celebrated in Salzheim, after which the young couple moved to Munich, where Leib already had an apartment. How her friends envied her! Not only was she marrying a Polish Jew, not only was it someone from her own town, but it was a match that her own father would have been pleased to make.

At the time of the wedding, Tziporah's husband was working for a religious Zionist organization, that having seemed to him the quickest way to get a visa to Palestine. Indeed, they were promised a legal certificate if he would only continue his work for another year, and they accepted. Thus, Tziporah was spared the experience of so many of her friends who went through Italy on the illegal immigration, of being caught by the British and interned on Cyprus.

Tziporah and her brother Mendel both succeeded in raising their children in their parents' tradition as Gerer *chassidim*. She now looks around at the prosperity of the Land of Israel, built with refugees and with reparations money. She is not surprised to see the tides of anti-Semitism rising again. Though Hitler's attempts to wipe out the Jewish people failed, many would have preferred to see him succeed. Of course, they are jealous when they see the Jews flourishing.

There is a more subtle catalyst to the Jew-hatred. She stood one day on a curb and watched as a man in a suit got into a Subaru and drove away. This would have been an entirely unremarkable event, except that, before sliding in behind the wheel, he threw the fringes of his woolen garment over his shoulder so they would not get in his way and folded up the tail of his long coat so it would not get wrinkled. There are people in the world who would be bothered to see a person in traditional Jewish dress who is sufficiently well-off to own a car.

The anti-Semites not only want to wipe out the Jews, they want to wipe out Jewishness. It must rankle them very much that in this period of prosperity, a religious Jew can have all the good things of this world without budging at all from the traditions of his fathers.

The
Soviet
Glacier

The progress of the fire varies with the wind, first eastward, then westward, then eastward again, to the part of the forest that had been buried many years before by a glacier. Though unable to conquer so vast a river of ice, the flames eat into the leading edge, licking at logs buried thirty years before. Steam and black smoke veil the entire area. Chunks of ice begin to fall from the projecting lip of the frozen wall. Finally, the entire face collapses, burying acts of blackened land. The avalanche exposes some of the seeds that had been locked in the ice for twenty-five years. A rain squall sweeps in from the west and, together with streams of water from the melting ice, extingiushes the blaze completely. The previously entrapped seeds are carried out of the glacier by the rain-fed rivulets.

FIRE AND ICE | 5

For the first two decades after the Revolution, most rabbis were allowed to retain their posts, though they and all loyal family members were denied many normal rights of citizenship. Etta Schapiro's father was not only the rabbi of a medium-sized city, he also had an underground *yeshivah*, and all the family's religious observances were carried on in secrecy. Etta grew up living the double life of a child in a religious family in Soviet Russia. Small wonder that Rabbi Schapiro had applied for an exit visa and asked a former student living in Palestine to arrange for a certificate to enter.

Tragically, just a short time before the papers arrived, Rabbi Schapiro died. The bitter event was made even more bitter by its shattering of Etta's long held dream of moving to the Land of Israel. The papers were only legal for the family if Rabbi Schapiro would be at their head.

A family council was held, and it was decided that one of

151

Etta's brothers, also a rabbi, would try to use them for himself and his family. The ages did not match at all, but perhaps the border guards would not pay so much attention to detail. The brother got out of Russia, into Palestine, and took a position as rabbi of the small settlement, the position that had been arranged for Etta's father.

Etta lived with her widowed mother, since her older sister and other brother were married and lived elsewhere. During the mass arrests of rabbis in 1937, her brother David was arrested.

For a political prisoner, the first stage after arrest is a lengthy interrogation that could stretch for months. At irregular intervals the prisoner is brought under guard to another building and asked a long series of questions, often repeated from one session to the next. He usually faces the same one or two interrogators, and notes are made of his answers. The prisoner tries to give acceptable, consistent answers which will not incriminate himself or his friends; the interrogator tries to catch him in an inconsistency or extract some admission of wrongdoing. The methods used depend on the case, interrogator and political climate, ranging from mild bully-buddy switches of tone up through extreme forms of physical torture. The more the interrogator knows of the truth, the harder it is for the prisoner to bluff his way through the ordeal. For Etta's brother David there was no unknown behind which to hide—his accuser was one of his best friends, turned communist.

David Schapiro was not summoned to his own trial. He only knew it was over when he was informed of the sentence: seven years of hard labor in Siberia. Before he was sent away his onetime friend, a former *yeshivah* student of his father, appeared at his cell door and was allowed in by the guard.

"I've come to ask you not to think badly of me for informing on you."

"How could I possibly think well of you?" asked David.

"You betrayed me, you betrayed my father, you betrayed the Torah . . ."

The other man began unbuttoning his shirt. "You know what the Talmud says about Chananiah, Mishael and Azariya. They had the strength to jump into the fiery furnace, but if they had been whipped they would have bowed down to the idol." He turned his back to David and raised his shirt, exposing a back of scarred stripes. He lowered his shirt and turned around to face David again. "I didn't do anything like that to you."

"The guards in Siberia will do it for you. Why is your blood redder than mine? Do you know that my wife and son will suffer while I'm gone?"

His former friend winced. "I had no choice," he protested.

"I don't believe you," said David flatly. "That you talked while being tortured I understand. But later, you must have had a choice between cooperating in the future or being sentenced."

"You can't imagine what it was like," said the other man, rebuttoning his shirt. "I hope you won't go through anything as painful." He took one last look at the unrelenting David and left the cell.

David was sent into exile.

In the thick of this latest crisis, a match was found for Etta. The religious underground spanned the entire Soviet Union, so the Shkolnik family in Voronezh, an industrial city south of Moscow, knew when a rabbi's daughter hundreds of miles away reached marriageable age, and Reb Yehudah Shkolnik travelled to meet her. They were married in her hometown, Etta moved to Voronezh, and her mother Leah moved to Moscow.

Voronezh had a vigorous, if hidden, Jewish community. Much of the burden of supporting it was borne by Reb Yehudah Shkolnik and his older brother Yosef, who were prominent Jewish industrialists.

How did the Shkolnik brothers become industrialists in

communist Russia, where all industries are the property of the State?

Before the Revolution, their father had been manager of vast tracts of forest he had leased from wealthy landowners. The brothers had salvaged much of the wealth they had inherited from him, in the form of buried gold and other inconspicuous assets. They had used these resources to set up a large knitwear factory. The enterprise officially belonged to the State, which took the profits, and the founders drew a regular salary as managers. The factory provided a large number of Jews with employment that did not require desecrating *Shabbos*.

Of course, they could not officially close the concern on Saturday, since that would be misuse of State property. Instead, in addition to their Jewish workers, they hired a certain number of Russians whose job it was to be on the premises in case of a surprise visit by a government inspection team. Since the Shkolniks did not want their non-Jewish workers to do work for them on *Shabbos*, they arranged for all the electricity in the building to be shorted out just before *Shabbos* arrived on Friday evenings. If an inspection team should arrive and find the Gentile workers sitting idle, the failure in the electricity would be an adequate explanation.

Even announced inspection tours were a source of danger. The Shkolniks were once informed that a delegation would be arriving to look over the factory on *Yom Kippur*. It was unthinkable that the managers be absent during a scheduled tour. They walked out of the synagogue early in the morning and hiked across the city, a journey of several hours, in their cloth shoes. The delegation was greeted affably, the visit passed without incident, and finally, the inspectors were escorted out. The two brothers then walked back across town, without having eaten or drunk anything since the previous evening, and rejoined the congregation.

The Shkolniks' charitable activities were on a scale with their business enterprise. They supported and concealed an entire Chabad *yeshivah*. Although the Shkolnik family was not *chassidic* in origin, Reb Yehudah was sympathetic to the movement's efforts, and Reb Yosef had gradually joined them. The clandestine *yeshivah* was housed in Reb Yehudah's summer bungalow, and Etta did the boys' laundry.

The Germans attacked Russia in June of 1941. After only a couple of months, the German troops were three-quarters of the way to Moscow. When refugees began pouring into Voronezh, it was only natural for the Shkolnik brothers to take a major role in providing for them. One Friday evening, when Reb Yosef lifted the silver cup full of wine, there was a pause, and then he set the cup down again.

"I can't do it," he announced to his family. "I can't recite *Kiddush* until I'm sure the refugees are taken care of."

He set off into the night and returned home only when he had arranged for food for all the travellers who had taken refuge in a nearby shelter.

One evening, a different sort of refugee appeared at Reb Yosef's door, one wearing a Red Army uniform. The soldier, a rabbi's son named Avram Chaiken, had been brought to Voronezh by a strange chain of circumstances. Seeking medical deferment from the front-line service, he had entered a clinic and had been examined by a female Jewish doctor who recognized the meaning of the four-cornered garment under his shirt. She wrote him a note saying that he was suffering from dormant tuberculosis, and at the very last hour before he was to be sent to the front, he was granted a month of sick leave. His hometown of Odessa had been evacuated, and he had been travelling eastward in search of his family when a lucky accident brought him to Voronezh, where a friend of his father's lived.

Avram's friend had brought him to Reb Yosef's blacked-out house, through streets in which German bombs were falling. Reb Yosef was sitting in a lighted inner room, studying a volume of the Talmud with his sons, when the visitor was announced. They invited Avram to take a seat, and he explained his situation.

"We will have to look for a way to get you a discharge from the army," said Reb Yosef. "Until we find it, you can live with us."

Etta took Avram's problem in hand. She had a cousin who had just finished his medical studies and had begun work in the army, serving in a clinic for the treatment of tuberculosis. She convinced him to issue Avram a certificate saying he was indeed suffering from that malady.

Avram also needed certification of the deferment by a certain military doctor on the Voronezh draft board. Reb Yehudah made contact with the doctor and offered him a substantial bribe, which Reb Yehudah and Reb Yosef paid out of their own pockets. The doctor might not have been willing to take the risk had it not been for the unsettled state of the draft office in Voronezh. The office was in great confusion, with all the files being packed up for shipment eastward, so the doctor saw little chance that he would ever get into trouble for issuing the requested document.

Avram still had a difficult task ahead of him—the job of finding his wife and children somewhere in the vastness of Russia. Since his steps had been so well guided up to this point, he had great hopes for future success. After consultation with the Shkolnik brothers, he decided that Tashkent, the capital of Uzbekistan, was the most likely place to begin his search. His uniform off, he caught a train going east.

In Voronezh, the bombing had intensified as the German troops drew nearer. The approaching Russian winter eventually halted the German advance, but Voronezh was in an exposed position. The government decided to evacuate the civilian population, and as much of the industrial equipment as possible, to the interior.

The Shkolniks had been preparing for such an eventuality, but there was only so much they could do. They had some liquid assets, and they converted whatever they could to gold, but the factory was not officially theirs, and no one was interested in buying their furniture and other movables. Most of their property would simply have to be abandoned. What gold they had would be difficult to transport, since it was illegal for private citizens to possess such valuable material. As the proverb current in post-Revolutionary Russia went, "Anyone who has gold, buries it in the ground. Anyone who does not, is himself buried in the ground." The evacuations would test the truth of that proverb.

KOMBASH, U.S.S.R. • 1941

The freight trains, lacking any water supplies or sanitation facilities for the suffering refugees loaded upon them, moved eastward through the cold and snow. Passenger cars could not be spared for the people, since they were all in use for transporting troops, and the crowding of people into the small cars threatened the spread of typhus through lice.

Some did not even reach the destination alive. One woman got off at a minor station to find drinking water for her family, and the train crew ignored her husband's pleas to wait for her before starting up again. Her family descended at the next stop and returned to the previous station, but she was not there. They widened their search and eventually found her fallen in the snow some distance down the track. Since she had no money, she had set off on foot to follow them. They brought her indoors and tried to revive her, but it was too late.

The group in which the Shkolniks were travelling was delivered to a small town named Kombash, whose houses were hollows scooped out of the soil and roofed over with sod. Reb Yosef continued on to Uzbekistan, while Reb Yehudah stayed behind in Kombash with his wife's family.

It was a large party that Reb Yehudah had under his protection in Kombash, including Etta's mother, the Shkolniks' two small daughters and Devorah and her children. Devorah's husband was not with them, because of the draft.

The first report they received from Uzbekistan was alarming. Reb Yosef and his family had come down with typhus almost immediately on arrival, and no one in the party was well enough to care for them. Since his own group was secure in Kombash, Reb Yehudah caught the next train to Tashkent to rescue his brother.

Reb Yehudah returned several weeks later, after Reb Yosef's branch of the family recovered. Having seen how poor the conditions were in Tashkent, he decided that they should attempt to settle in Kazakhstan instead. He took Etta with him to help find employment and an apartment, leaving her mother and Devorah with the children in Kombash.

When he and Etta arrived in Alma-Ata, the capital of Kazakhstan, they found that other religious Jews had preceded them. One, a Chabad *chassid* named Shneur Rotner, agreed to accept mail for them, so they sent his address to the family in Kombash.

At the end of his first day of searching for a job, the usually efficient Reb Yehudah returned rather discouraged to their room. He had a headache, he felt tired, and he had not accomplished much. When he awoke the next morning the headache was still with him, he felt lethargic, and his temperature was rising. Having just nursed his brother's family through typhus, he did not need to wait for the rash to develop in order to realize what was wrong. He was soon delirious and unable to make any efforts on his own behalf. The burden of managing everything fell on his capable wife.

Etta went to the hospital to get Reb Yehudah admitted. The facilities were severely overcrowded, and at first, the administration turned her away. Most of Etta's reserve of cash had to be used up just to obtain admittance papers.

The treatment for typhus at the time was adequate nutrition during the two-week period of high fever which characterizes the disease. Because of the famine in Russia that winter, the hospital could not or would not provide the needed bland cereals. Etta had to procure them on the black market, and within a short time, all her money was gone.

Meeting one of their new acquaintances on the street, she asked him for a loan.

"I'm sorry," answered the man. "I haven't got any money right now."

Etta turned away, discouraged. The acquaintance noticed her wedding ring, which was a thick, gold one.

"Wait," he said, calling her back. "If you want, I can buy that ring from you."

So he *did* have money!

Etta turned on him in fury.

"You know I need this money to save my husband's life, and yet you wouldn't loan it to me. Let me tell you, if you were the only person in the world who would buy this ring, I would throw it in the river before I would sell it to you!"

Etta returned to the hospital in a bitter mood. She had not thought of selling her ring, but in no way would she sell it to that insensitive man. She would find someone else to whom to sell it. Meanwhile, there was another problem. Although she still had some cereal and milk left, there was no fire on which to heat it. She took some wood from a wood pile in the courtyard of the hospital and built a fire. The pricks from her conscience over stealing the wood only added to her misery.

As the first week came to an end, Etta waited anxiously for the slight drop in temperature which often signals a non-fatal case of the disease. But Reb Yehudah's fever remained stubbornly high. The anticipated day of crisis at the end of two weeks began to approach, and Etta remained by her husband's bed as much as possible. One afternoon, as she sat there unobtrusively, she overheard two of the nurses talking.

"They've admitted another patient," reported one of them.

"Another patient? Where in the world will we put him?"

"Well, for the moment, we've made him a temporary cot in the hall, and after tonight, you know . . ." She gestured significantly in the direction of Reb Yehudah's bed.

"Ah, yes," said the other nurse. "Of course."

Etta was close to despair. The hospital staff expected him to die that very night. Was there nothing she could do to save him? She left the hospital and went to Shneur Rotner's house to ask his advice.

"A letter just arrived for you," he told her as she entered.

Etta took the envelope. It was from Uzbekistan, forwarded from Kombash. She tore open the seal and found that it came from Avram Chaiken, the soldier for whom they had arranged the draft deferment. He wrote to her husband that he had found his family near starvation in a town close to Tashkent. After thanking the Shkolniks for their help, he ended the letter with a blessing. "Just as you have helped reunite a father with his children, may you merit to be a father to your children for many years to come."

Etta rushed back to her husband's bedside with the letter in her hand. Slipping it under his pillow, she added her own prayer that the blessing would come true. If it was not destined to be fulfilled, why had it arrived at just this critical moment?

Etta left the hospital again, sold her wedding ring and bought some butter. She located the doctor treating her husband and requested that he remain at her husband's side that night. She gave him the butter as a present. He accepted the gift and remained with his patient. That night was a tense one. Finally, near morning, the patient's fever began to drop, suddenly descending from one hundred and four degrees to almost normal. Reb Yehudah would recover.

ALMA-ATA, U.S.S.R.

After Reb Yehudah recuperated, he and Etta brought the rest of the family over from Kombash. The government allocated a bread ration to each refugee, but the famine was so severe that the bread often ran out before everyone on line received their ration. Etta used to take the girls to the fields in which potatoes or carrots had been harvested, where they would all dig in the ground in hope of finding a small tuber missed by the harvesters. In later years, the girls remembered the adventure of digging for potatoes more than the suffering from hunger. But, their mother could not forget the times when her children begged for something to eat, and she had nothing to give them.

Eventually, the adults found employment, but the situation was not much alleviated. Though they had money, there was no food available to buy. Rebbetzin Leah, Etta's mother, cared for the children each day while her daughters worked, and she was in charge of allocating the family's small bread ration at lunchtime. One afternoon, Etta's younger daughter Raizel left the room for a moment, first placing her slice of bread on the window sill. Her cousin Shlomo, finding a stray piece of bread lying on the window sill, decided to eat it first and leave questions for later. When Raizel returned, she found her lunch missing. Rebbetzin Leah, with nothing at all to give her in its place, expressed such anger at Shlomo that the other children, even Raizel, felt sorry for the boy.

Reb Yehudah set to work to secure the basic necessities of Jewish life, including kosher food, employment that would not require working on *Shabbos* and *Yom Tov*, and a Jewish education for his daughters. The art of skillful bribing lies in knowing whom to bribe, with how much, how often. The Shkolniks' Jewish acquaintances in town suggested a preliminary group of bribable officials. Each had a friend a step or two higher up in the ranks. Eventually, Reb Yehudah established connections with someone able to appoint him as manager of a knitwear factory. By the time he reached this level, the stakes were quite high, and throughout his tenure at the post, he provided the responsible official with firewood, cooking gas, table delicacies and clothing.

Although the factory provided Reb Yehudah with a position in the city and patronage to dispense, the actual factory manager's salary was quite small. In order to supplement his income, Reb Yehudah opened a second, smaller factory in his own yard. The laborers were Gentile women, who produced various sorts of socks and stockings. This factory, too, was registered as belonging to the government. However, it produced some stockings made with black market yarn, and these were sold on the black market. The profit from these side transactions paid the extra expenses incurred by observing Jewish law.

The secret police, going at the time under the initials NKVD, had its suspicions of Reb Yehudah and searched the house and yard frequently. The family maintained a state of constant alert against these visits. Whenever someone would spot the NKVD men approaching from afar, Etta would take her gold watch and Reb Yehudah's, items too valuable for private citizens to possess legally, and would slip them into the dress of her oldest daughter Nechamah. The little girl would then be sent out into the street to play until after the unwelcome visitors had left.

A Jewish family's Gentile maid was the usual informant to the police about illegal activities. The Shkolniks' non-Jewish maid, a Russian orphan by the name of Malasha, had grown up in Rebbetzin Leah's household and had entered Reb Yehudah's household after his marriage to Etta. He used to say that other people upon marriage received a monetary dowry, which quickly disappeared. He had gotten a dowry he could not get rid of.

Malasha, though sharp-tongued, was devoted to the family and had grown quite knowledgeable about Jewish law. One day, Raizel noticed a knife handle sticking out of the ground in the yard. She asked Malasha what it was doing there.

"Oh, that," said Malasha with a disdainful sniff. "Your 'righteous' neighbor came waltzing in here, hacked off a chunk of butter with one of our *fleishige* knives and walked out again without so much as a by-your-leave. I put the knife in the ground to make it kosher again."

It was Malasha who taught the girls the blessings over different types of food, leading them through the Hebrew text of the blessings word by word. Although Malasha could neither read nor write, she did speak Yiddish and knew those Hebrew prayers the little girls were expected to say by heart before they were old enough to read. Malasha also saw to it that the girls washed their hands and said *Modeh Ani* when they woke up in the morning. Any laziness on the part of her charges was greeted with great scorn. "This one is a *shikseh*! She doesn't want to wash her hands!"

During one of their searches of the house, the NKVD decided to take Malasha into their offices for interrogation.

Since nothing that went on in the household was unknown to Malasha, even an unintentional slip on her part could cause considerable trouble, and if she were talked into betraying the Shkolniks, they were lost.

Reb Yehudah and Etta were standing in a different room from Malasha and the policemen. Etta raised her voice and said to Reb Yehudah in Yiddish, "Malasha better watch her tongue. If she says anything to the police, I don't envy her. I don't envy her at all."

Malasha was marched off with the NKVD men, and the family waited tensely at home to see if Reb Yehudah would be arrested. At last, Malasha returned, alone.

"I didn't tell them anything," she said gruffly to Etta. "I was more afraid of you than I was of them."

The Gentile women who worked at the home factory, however, did not have the same affection for the family as did Malasha, nor the same compunctions about getting their employer into trouble. This manifested itself when Reb Yehudah hired a Jewish refugee from Poland to be a guard in the home factory. (It was an act of charity. The real guard of the factory was a large dog named Silva, and the Polish Jew actually slept through most of his watch.) He was a ritual slaughterer by trade, and (when he wasn't asleep) he would sit on a bench outside the factory sharpening his slaughtering knife, which had to be completely free of nicks. He would come on duty just as the Russian knitters would go off duty.

One day, the police appeared at the door, demanding that Reb Yehudah turn over to them the murderer he was harboring on his premises. It took Reb Yehudah a while to figure out whom they were referring to. Even after he realized that his workers had taken fright of the guard and reported him as a murderer, he still had to concoct some sort of story, since sharpening a ritual slaughtering knife was not considered a respectable pastime in Stalinist Russia.

There were other sources of danger. They secretly baked *matzah* for *Pesach*. The Shkolniks paid a Gentile double rent for the period they used his isolated cellar, once for use of the cellar and once to keep him silent. The owner thought they were preparing food for some innocent family celebration, but he realized it was not entirely legal. The *matzah* was prepared with attention to every detail of the law. The water was removed from a well after sundown, each batch was mixed, rolled and baked within eighteen minutes, and so forth. There was an extra element of haste, however, because the whole operation had to be finished before someone noticed unusual activity in the cellar and reported it.

Then there was the synagogue, also in a basement, but one rented all year round. Some Jewish neighborhoods in Alma-Ata had daily services, but in their suburban village, there were only fifteen to twenty Jewish families, so they held services only on *Shabbos* and holidays. They also built a secret *mikveh*, hidden under a trap-door in the floor of the Tashtag synagogue. On *Simchas Torah*, the children were kept from dancing in that part of the room, so that they wouldn't notice the hollowness of the floor.

The secret religious activities were always in danger of being discovered. One holiday, as the congregants stood wrapped in their *talleisim,* someone nervously pointed to the cellar window. On the other side of it was a pair of army boots, which had come to a stop in the stretch of ground outside, near the only entrance to the synagogue. There was no way the congregants could escape without attracting attention. They stood in careful, tense silence. Steps descended the cellar stairs and a Red Army officer entered the room. He looked around the room full of frozen faces, many of them bearded.

"Don't be afraid of me," he said. "I won't turn you in. I am here because I want you to help me."

"What do you need?" asked one of the leaders of the group, considerably calmed.

"Today is my mother's *yahrzeit*. I want someone to say *Kaddish* for her."

The Shkolnik family was haunted by the fear that Reb Yehudah would be arrested and exiled. The factory, the *matzos*, the synagogue—there were so many ways he was vulnerable to an informer. At last, the police did show up to make an arrest. Ironically, though, it was not Reb Yehudah they took, but Etta.

Reb Yehudah had taken pity on some refugees who had no work and had delegated to them the task of selling the illegal products of the home factory on the black market. Not being particularly skillful, they attracted the attention of the police and were arrested. They confessed to engaging in black market transactions and indicated the Shkolniks as their source of merchandise. The police, perhaps a bit wary of Reb Yehudah's connections, chose to arrest Etta in place of her husband.

Etta was put in jail and interrogated in the hope she would confess and implicate her husband as well. She was steadfast in refusing to admit any guilt, insisting that the merchandise had been part of the legal production quota of the factory. She claimed to have invoices at home which would prove as much. Since Etta was a forceful and persuasive woman, she eventually introduced enough doubt into the minds of her interrogators that they agreed to allow her to go home with a police escort and produce the appropriate invoices. Thus it was that Reb Yehudah answered a knock at the door to find his wife with a policeman on either side.

Although Reb Yehudah had been engaged in intensive efforts to free his wife ever since her arrest, he had not, of course, been allowed to speak to her. He had no idea what story she might have told them, so he maintained a noncommittal silence and waited for some cue from Etta as to the role he was to play. The cue came immediately.

"I've had some difficulty convincing these comrades that the stockings they think are contraband were really produced legally. We've come to find the invoices."

"The invoices? Certainly. I have them in the files."

The Shkolniks' house consisted of two rooms, a large one which served as kitchen, living room and dining room, and a back room where the family slept. Reb Yehudah led the visitors to the back room and took out some files relating to his business affairs. He knew roughly what items had been in the batch of knitwear that the police had confiscated from their agents. He tried to find a document which could be quickly altered to give the proper description. The policemen followed Reb Yehudah into his study, still keeping Etta between them. Reb Yehudah actually extracted the document he needed from the first file he opened, but he made a pretense of further searching while signalling to Etta. She distracted the attention of the men for a moment while Reb Yehudah added a few words to the invoice and changed the estimated value. Then he slipped the paper into the file he was holding and waited until both policemen were looking at him again. At that point, he "found" the document.

The forged invoice passed the policemen's inspection. One was delegated to bring it to headquarters so that their superiors could be convinced as well. Meanwhile, the other stayed to keep his eye on Etta until the charges were officially dropped. The Shkolniks invited him to lunch with them. After a plate of warm food and a glass of vodka, the man relaxed considerably, and his eyes began to wander idly around the room. At last, his gaze rested on Reb Yehudah's shoes, which were quite new. Good shoes were hard to get during the war years.

"Why don't we trade?" suggested Reb Yehudah, radiating comradely spirit.

"What a fine idea!" agreed the policeman enthusiastically.

The two men exchanged shoes, another vodka was poured and the atmosphere grew yet more convivial. After some more friendly chatting, the policeman stood up to go.

"I'm sure your wife will be cleared, so I see no point in remaining here to guard her. It was pleasant making your acquaintance, and perhaps we shall meet again."

"Under more pleasant circumstances, I hope we shall," agreed Reb Yehudah, rising and showing his guest to the door.

In the following months, the Shkolniks developed a fine working relationship with that policeman, a relationship that proved helpful for other Jews of the city on other occasions.

The NKVD was only one source of fear for the Shkolniks. The other was the subverting influence of outside pressures upon their daughters' religious education. Before the Revolution, most of the Jews in Russia had been religious, but it was extremely unusual to find any child educated in Soviet schools who remained faithful. If they wanted to guard their grandchildren from assimilation, they had to teach their daughters everything as fully as they themselves had learned it. They could not be content with passing on a minimum of basic observances. If each generation is less religious than the previous one, it does not take long for a family to lose the entire tradition.

Their first concern was to keep the girls out of the state schools, but to do this required guile on the girls' part. Every morning, from the time they reached school age, the two girls put their school bags on their backs and walked out of the house acting quite cheerily, waving good-bye to their family. But instead of turning in the direction of the local school, they set off on a track through the woods. If anyone questioned them, they had a well-rehearsed story of an aunt who taught in a neighboring village school, in which they were registered. Once they were deep in the woods, they returned on a different track and entered their courtyard through a back gate. They remained shut indoors and out of prying neighbors' sight all morning, and at the end of school hours, they reversed the route. The whole performance was put on without fail twice a day, every day. One never knew how watchful the neighbors might be.

Reb Yehudah hired anyone he could find who might have something to teach the girls. He issued them papers as guards in the factory. One of their teachers was a *yeshivah* boy from Poland, whose entire family had been wiped out by the murderous Germans. He would speak for hours of the destruction of the Temple and other catastrophes suffered by the Jewish people. Perhaps it assuaged some of his own grief to remember that he was not alone in witnessing a widespread destruction and surviving it. He ended his stories, which held the girls' attention throughout, on a note of hope, as he looked forward to the future redemption in the Messiah's days. He sang to the girls a song of yearning for Jerusalem, and they were soon staunchly convinced that they would rather live in a hovel in the Holy Land than in a palace in Russia.

Their teacher for *Beraishis,* an elderly man named Reb Ephraim, was absolutely fearless about keeping the commandments in public. He walked through the streets of Alma-Ata in the same long coat, beard and sidelocks that he had always worn. The Russian children would taunt him in the street, calling out, "Hey, Grandpa, why did you put on Grandma's dress?"

"She went off in my clothes, and I had nothing else to wear," Reb Ephraim would reply good-naturedly.

Whatever the girls learned, they were expected to commit to memory. Books were scarce, and their parents never knew when the next upheaval might close this relatively peaceful period in their lives and separate them from their children altogether. This might be the only chance the girls would ever have to learn the story of the binding of Yitzchak, or of Yaakov's dreams.

It was a difficult regimen for the girls. There were long hours to be filled every morning, with no opportunity to take a break and play outside. Their tutors were not, in general, professional teachers, and they had as educational materials only the family prayerbook, a copy of *Beraishis* and one or two other texts.

Their cousin Minna, their Aunt Devorah's daughter, suffered a different set of pressures. She was somewhat older than the Shkolnik girls, and after the first year in Alma-Ata, Devorah had been forced to enroll her in school. Etta and Devorah went to speak to Minna's teacher, a Gentile. They explained that on Saturdays Minna would have to stay home to help her mother with the housework, because Minna's grandmother, who lived with them, was old-fashioned about her religion and did not do housework on *Shabbos*. This reasonable-sounding story, accompanied by a generous bribe, satisfied Minna's teacher, and Minna was allowed to stay home on *Shabbos*, making up the work later. The story did not satisfy Minna's Jewish fellow pupils, though, who teased her constantly about her religion. Minna's only friends were her young cousins and several Gentile girls her own age who had great respect for her religious practices.

The Shkolnik girls, with only each other as companions, occupied themselves with whatever activities their parents could arrange for them. Some variety in their lives was provided by the pageantry of the Jewish holidays, such activities as cleaning the house before *Pesach*, gathering greens for *Shavuos* and decorating the *sukkah* for *Sukkos*.

On *Chanukah*, Reb Yehudah would take the *Chanukah menorah*, fill it with oil, set it on the window sill and light it, but he would first close and latch the heavy storm shutters, so that no ray of light would escape the house. The purpose of lighting the *menorah* in the window is so people outside can see it, something Reb Yehudah dared not allow, but he wanted his daughters to know that it should be lit in the window.

While the candles were burning, Reb Yehudah and Etta would tell the girls stories from the whole span of Jewish history. One theme recurred constantly—that in each generation enemies rose up to kill the Jews or attempt to prevent them from observing the Torah, but always the Jews continued to be faithful to the religion of their fathers. The four Shkolniks sang songs together, not happy songs about spinning tops, but slow, sad songs about the suffering of the Jewish people.

> Oh, you shining lights so small,
> Now you tell me tales that thrall,
> > Stories from so long ago.
> You tell me of a bloody fight,
> Of heroism and of might,
> > Wonders from so long ago.
>
> And as I watch you glimmering,
> > A memory comes shimmering,
> > There speaks an ancient dream.
> "Jew, you once fought so glorious,
> And Jew, you were victorious."
> > How strange it all does seem!
>
> Oh, you shining lights so small,
> How the tales you tell do thrall,
> > And rouse my pain, make me perplexed!
> From his dreams, the Jew awakes,
> From his prayers, a question quakes,
> > "O, G-d, what will happen next?"

Etta felt the full, tragic weight of Jewish history pressing heavily on her two small girls. To the west lay Poland, where Jews were being murdered by the thousands daily. To the east lay Siberia, where their uncle shivered and starved for seven long years. Ahead of them lay concealment and deception, forged papers and fear of discovery. At least the children would know that they were not the first and only Jews to suffer.

All their teachers were well-taught in suffering, but there was one whose pain made a particularly sharp impression on both Nechamah and Raizel. Professor Millman, as the girls called him, was the only non-observant Jew that Reb Yehudah had hired to teach the girls. He was one of those Jews who had once worked to convert the Jews to atheism. Millman had been a man of two loves, communism and Zionism, to each of which he had devoted a part of his life. In his youth, he had emigrated to Palestine and had been active among the Zionist leaders there, urging them to place their trust in Russia rather than in the Western nations. Eventually, he decided that the universal appeal of communism outweighed his particularist loyalty to the Land of Israel and the Jewish people. A few years in Stalinist Russia thoroughly disillusioned him about communism, but it was too late to return to his other love. The authorities would not issue him an exit visa to return to Palestine.

Millman was well-educated and taught during the war at the university in Alma-Ata. He tried to use his influence on the Jewish students to sway them toward Zionism. It was a dangerous step. Like religious Jews, Zionists were very vulnerable to political exile. Eventually, he lost his teaching position. Reb Yehudah noticed him one day on the streets of Alma-Ata, an educated-looking Jew in worn clothing and torn shoes. As an act of charity, Reb Yehudah invited Millman home for lunch and learned all about his situation. The story Millman told left his host in a quandary. Reb Yehudah felt terribly sorry for him and would have liked to help him in some way, but since Millman would not take outright charity, he would have to be hired to do some job. The obvious job was that of teaching the girls Hebrew, but what would be the point of going to great lengths to keep them out of communist schools if he gave them an atheist as a teacher?

As Reb Yehudah grew better acquainted with the impoverished professor, his warmer impulses prevailed, and he did give the job to Millman. It was a considerable inconvenience for the family, because some adult always had to be around during Millman's lessons to monitor his presentation of the material. Etta made an advance agreement with him that he would not say anything at variance with the girls' religious education.

From an academic point of view, the arrangement was a very successful one. Millman knew a great deal, and all his pent-up love for Hebrew language and culture was poured out on his two young pupils, who were five and seven at the time. He not only taught them grammar and vocabulary, but also instilled in them his own longing for the Land of Israel. That was acceptable to the Shkolniks. After all, whence did Millman inherit that yearning, if not from his religious parents and grandparents?

One of the Hebrew poems he taught the girls was poignantly descriptive of his own tragic situation. Nechamah and Raizel learned it by heart, though the meaning was beyond them:

> At the crossroads stands a tree,
> > Withered and distressed.
> Across the sea I have a land,
> > How can I find rest?

> At the crossroads stands a tree,
> > Its branches bare and dry.
> If I return not to that land.
> > From longing I will die.

Millman respected his agreement with Etta in principle, but in practice he did not always find it easy to keep. One day, while they were speaking about the Land of Israel, Nechamah made a contribution.

"Mommy says that if you walk past Rachel's tomb, you hear Rachel crying for her exiled children."

"That isn't true," said Millman. "I walked past Rachel's tomb once when I lived in Palestine, and I didn't hear anyone crying."

The girls reported this to their mother as a new piece of information about the world. "You know, Mommy, the professor says that he walked past Rachel's tomb and didn't hear her crying for her children."

"Tell me," asked Etta. "Do you remember what I told you about Rivkah, and how the twins fought in her womb? When she walked past a hall of Torah study, Yaakov would struggle to get out, and when she walked past a temple for idol worship, Esau wanted to leave."

"We remember," the girls assured her.

"Each one felt the place that echoed the yearnings of his own soul. The same thing happens with Rachel's tomb. If the person walking past is crying in his own heart over the exile of the Divine Presence, then he can hear Rachel crying. The professor is not crying in his heart over the exile of the Divine Presence, so he hears nothing."

The girls, pleased to hear their mother's version vindicated, carried this answer back to the professor. The answer impressed him, and to the girls he admitted defeat, but his feelings were hurt. After the lesson, he sought out Etta to complain about having his status lowered in the eyes of his pupils. Etta was more than ready to confront him, since her own protest was a matter of principle, not of pique.

"If someone delivers to you the keys of a closet," she told

him, "and trusts you to guard it, you shouldn't abuse that trust. It would be wrong for you to upset the piles, or take out some piece of clothing. You agreed not to interfere with what we taught the girls before you began the job."

Professor Millman apologized. His position as the lone atheist in a religious household was at times inconvenient for his hosts, but it was yet more unsettling for Millman. What he saw of life in the Shkolniks' house was so at variance with his prejudices about Orthodox Judaism that those prejudices were eventually destroyed. He found Reb Yehudah sophisticated, charming and selfless. There was a long and painful distance between admiring Reb Yehudah and adopting his way of life, but eventually Millman started moving in that direction.

The former atheist began donning *tefillin* every morning. After a while, he began to pray in a *tallis* and to keep kosher. Eventually, *Shabbos* observance followed, and the matter did not end with his own change of heart. He began bringing former students to enjoy the festival meals at Reb Yehudah's table. Professor Millman had discovered the source of his own idealism, and he wished to share that discovery with others.

MOSCOW, U.S.S.R.

M illman was not the only Jew to move closer to Judaism during the war years. Although the finality of the Final Solution was not known in Russia until some time after the war, it was at least clear from Nazi propaganda that the Jews had been singled out for severe persecutions. Many Russian Jews who thought they had assimilated completely began to wonder about this Jewishness which seemed to separate them so permanently and inescapably from other peoples.

In Alma-Ata, these feelings were heightened by the arrival

of the righteous and erudite scholar Rav Levi Yitzchak Schneerson, a relative by marriage of the Lubavitcher Rebbe. He was ransomed from exile through the efforts of a group of Chabad *chassidim* centered in Tashtag. Although physically broken by five years of exile, his spirit was undaunted, and he revolutionized many Jewish lives during the four months he lived in Alma-Ata until his death. Etta's brother, who returned from his own exile the same year, wrote a description of the funeral:

Silent strode the mourners, each as if walking innocently to his work. These are bureaucrats, workers, exiles. Each glances to the sides to see if anyone notices him in his misdemeanor, if anyone sees that he is following the coffin. Deep in one's heart the terrible pain is buried, together with the fear and the anxiety about anyone knowing about this, about suffering punishment on this account.

The last *Kaddish*, recited by an elderly Chabad *chassid*, broke the hearts of the mourners, who choked tight the well-springs of tears. The terror preying in this miserable land those many years had spread its fearful wings so wide that even the funeral of a rabbi could have been judged a counter-revolutionary demonstration and its participants made to pay for this "crime" with years of imprisonment and exile.

Thus passed away the distinguished man, the great rabbi who stood, with the stubbornness of flint, between the straits of the grave and the depths of the pit, holding his position in a large congregation, not surrendering to the sea of despair whose destructive waves beat from all sides on the tattered remnant of Torah Jewry in Russia. Perhaps the day will come and someone will be found who can describe the daily self-sacrifice of this final captain over the glorious Jewry of Russia, the last of leaders who fought inside a furnace from which there was no salvation, an upright man, never bowing under the impure hand.

Special among them was the last rabbi of the great congregation of Yekaterinislav, the righteous and erudite scholar Rav Levi Yitzchak Schneerson.

After Rav Levi Yitzchak's passing, his wife Rebbetzin Chanah Meyerovna had continued to live in Alma-Ata. She became a close friend of Rebbetzin Leah Shkolnik and her two daughters. Rebbetzin Chanah would visit their house, and the very image of nobility, she would hold marvelous conversations with Rebbetzin Leah, Etta and Devorah, conversations of intelligent and educated women, teachers all of them, dedicated to educating a new generation of loyal Jews. In addition to personal friendship, Devorah had an extra tie to Rebbetzin Chanah, for her husband Dov Ber Gershgoren was a Chabad *chassid* and Rebbetzin Chanah's son was married to the Lubavitcher Rebbe's only daughter.

The war moved toward its conclusion. The Red Army was advancing all along the front, and the evacuated territories were being resettled. Religious Jews began moving back to the Western cities, reestablishing the Jewish communities in Moscow and other places.

Devorah and her husband, who were among the first to leave Alma-Ata, decided to move back to Moscow. Before leaving, Devorah pressed Rebbetzin Chanah to come as well, promising to find her a place to stay as soon as they would get settled. All the swirl of activity around Rav Levi Yitzchak during his brief career in Alma-Ata had attracted the NKVD's attention, and she was constantly under surveillance. The secret police kept close watch over anyone bearing the name Schneerson, and Devorah felt Rebbetzin Chanah was not safe as long as the secret police could reach her so easily. Others in the Alma-Ata Chabad community felt the same way, and eventually convinced Rebbetzin Chanah to go underground and seek a way to meet up with her son Rav Menachem Mendel in New York. She left

Alma-Ata for Moscow several months after Devorah and her family.

The Shkolniks, however, had no particular plans to move within Russia. To move a business, particularly if it does not officially belong to you, is very difficult. But it was saddening for them to watch as their fellow Jews began moving out of Kazakhstan and Uzbekistan in the direction of the capital.

One day, early in 1946, a Polish refugee who often came by to collect charity from Reb Yehudah appeared at the door and asked to speak to Etta. The girls knew him well. Whenever the guard dog Silva produced a litter of puppies, this man would carry them off "for his grandchildren." Etta knew that he really planned to sell them on the black market as watchdogs. The girls, before they too caught on, called him the "grandfather of the puppies."

On this occasion, the "grandfather of the puppies" was interested in a different and more serious sort of business proposition. He had in his possession Polish identity papers for a Polish family consisting of a husband, a wife and two daughters. Perhaps the Shkolniks were interested in buying them? Etta hesitated over the decision. The price was high, and there was the usual danger that this might be a trap set to incriminate them. On the other hand, the war had ended, and there were disturbing signs that the secret police might be planning to clamp down on religious Jews who stayed in the country. After considerable deliberation, Etta weighed out the full price in gold and took the papers.

When Reb Yehudah arrived home that evening, he applauded her decision. The risk in trying to cross the border was tremendous, but the reward, freedom to raise their children as religious Jews, outweighed the danger. Reb Yehudah turned his full attention to this project. As usual, he planned in quantity. It was not enough to save his own family. He wanted to help his friends, family and neighbors escape, too. Since each set of Polish papers was expensive, he rushed to liquidate his assets to raise money for the scheme. He had a limited time in which to work. The repatriation transports would begin in the summer and continue through December.

Rebbetzin Chanah, who could leave the country only in a way by which no officials would see her face, first moved to Moscow without registering her presence. But being under surveillance, her disappearance was immediately noted, and she had to assume that the NKVD was looking for her. For the early part of her stay in Moscow she moved from one Chabad household to the next, never staying in the same place twice. Finally, early in the summer, Devorah located a war widow who was short of money and was willing to put up Devorah's "aunt" without registering her in the residents' book. The exorbitant rent was paid by some of the wealthier members of the Moscow Chabad community.

Since Rebbetzin Chanah was a well-known personage, it was dangerous for her to appear on the streets. The secret police was constantly trying to recruit agents from the Chabad community. The method was simple. They collected evidence against someone, arrested him and offered him the choice between going into exile or working for them.

"Listen, comrade," said one such interrogator to his victim. "I have spoken with you a great deal, and I have gotten to know you well. I recognize that you are an honest man, faithful and good-hearted. I am forced to confess the truth and admit that the [secret police] has gotten a reputation as a horrible institution. This is only because we lack honest and forthright personnel. For this reason, I would like to offer you a position with us. You won't have to sit here in the [secret police] offices. No, no. You can continue to work at your regular employment, making your shoelaces. You can continue to behave just as you always have, to go to the synagogue to pray and so forth. What will be your job? Once a month you will go to a certain place and tell someone what you heard in the synagogue, what subjects people were discussing, what certain people did, and so on . . . No one will ever know. For this, we will release you from jail. You will return to your wife, to your four children. You will be free from taxes. You will get a bonus and other nice things that will surprise you. Well, comrade, do you agree? You can be released immediately."

"I would gladly accept your offer, but I just can't. The sort of work you describe requires a sociable person, whereas I am a quiet type who never mixes with people," lied the prisoner. "If you asked me to make you a pair of shoes I might try, but I would botch the job. I'm not a cobbler."

With those words, he saved himself from betraying his friends and instead spent three years of exile in the Urals, while his wife went blind from overwork. This man had the strength to refuse, but others, particularly those on the outer fringes of the religious community, did not. The agents were usually recognized within a few months by a tendency to ask questions irrelevant to the current discussion and a habit of sidling up to listen to other people's conversations. In the meantime, however, they could cause a lot of damage, and even after they were recognized, they were still a nuisance and a danger.

Rebbetzin Chanah had to be kept away from any such informant. To keep her out of stores, Devorah's daughter Minna did the shopping every day. *Shabbosim* she passed at Devorah's house. She wanted to apply for a legal exit permit, but eventually her *chassidim* convinced her that it would never be granted. She resigned herself to the necessity of crossing the border illegally, as soon as it could be arranged.

Around the same time, the summer of 1946, Rebbetzin Leah arrived in Moscow with her granddaughters Nechamah and

Raizel. The Shkolniks had decided to send the girls ahead for the summer vacation, so that the family would not arouse suspicion in Alma-Ata by departing all together at once.

A number of Chabad families had travelled directly to Lemberg, from where the repatriation transports were scheduled to begin soon. With the aid of the local Jewish community, activists among the *chassidim* managed to obtain passports for a significantly sized group, and they crossed the border safely in one of the first transports. The head of the Lemberg community went away on a trip, but one of the leaders of the Chabad group, Zev Manevitch, secured passports through other channels. A second group was sent off and crossed the border safely.

News of the successes spread quickly to the Chabad communities in other parts of Russia, and more families arrived in Lemberg every day. The poorer families borrowed money from their wealthier friends to pay for Polish documents, and a third group prepared to set out. Zev Manevitch was planning to leave with this group. Since the head of the local community had just returned from his trip, Zev called on him to say good-bye and to thank him for all his previous assistance.

"No, don't go! You'll all be arrested. The police have found out about what you are doing," declared the other man.

Zev realized that the community leader must have been interrogated by the secret police, now called the MGB, about their activities.

"What should I do?" Zev asked.

"Take a taxi and go around to all your people to warn them to stay off those trains," the leader replied. "The government is planning to send armed men to arrest them all after they have already set out."

Was that a genuine warning from a friend, or the planted suggestion of an MGB agent to keep them in place? Either way, it was clear that the police were on to them. Zev ordered a taxi and began to make the rounds in Lemberg on his mission of warning. The train waited two days for its extra passengers, but the Chabad contingent did not appear. The head of the Lemberg community continued to warn them that it was a trap.

A telegram with a veiled warning was sent to the Chabad community in Moscow and other parts of Russia: RELATIVES IN LEMBERG HAVE FALLEN ILL. The movement of families to Lemberg halted completely, and for the month preceding *Rosh Hashanah*, the situation remained static. The plight of the families in Lemberg was dismal. In order to avoid attracting unwelcome attention from the police, they had not registered legally. They had to pay very high rents, for a landlord whose tenants were not registered with the house committee could suffer serious consequences if caught. The bearded men also stayed indoors to avoid attracting attention. They had paid out large sums for the passports, which had now been cancelled, and many had no funds for a protracted and expensive illegal stay in Lemberg. On the other hand, with freedom so close, it was hard to give up and go back to Moscow.

The leaders of the group organized themselves into a committee to deal with the situation. They raised money to support the families in Lemberg, continued to search out channels for the purchase of Polish passports and sent agents to other border towns in search of alternate routes to the West. Women, boys and unbearded men were pressed into service as messengers, and the headquarters of the committee was kept a secret from all but those actually working for the committee. The leaders themselves made a pact not to leave until they had gotten exit visas for the families in their care. In distributing passports, first priority was given to young people and families with small children whose Jewish education was at stake. Families were mixed and matched to fit the papers available. All the documents in the world, though, would not help as long as the people were afraid to set foot in the trains.

When the crisis broke in Lemberg, Rebbetzin Chanah was placed in a particularly difficult position. If she could not flee the country, her chances of remaining hidden from the police were small. Her case was taken up by one of the heroines of the period, a woman known as *die Muma Sarah* or Aunt Sarah.

Sarah Katzenellenbogen was a widow of great talent and energy. Originally a businesswoman, she later began devoting her talents to protecting and liberating her co-religionists. She would appear occasionally in Alma-Ata during the war years, swathed in a large gray wool cape. In pockets under the cape, she concealed documents she was carrying from one place to another to help exiles, prisoners or others threatened by the police. During the Lemberg period, she was active in sending children and *yeshivah* students across the border.

Her activities were so widespread that she expected the police would eventually catch on to her. For this reason, she had obtained a forged passport, which she kept always on hand to enable her to escape the country in time. But *die Muma Sarah* was from a Chabad family, and out of concern for the safety of Rebbetzin Chanah, she surrendered her own passport to the other woman. Rebbetzin Chanah left Moscow on *Rosh Hashanah*, passing through Lemberg, where she had to keep her presence a secret both from the MGB and from the Chabad *chassidim*. After seven days of final arrangements in Lemberg, she boarded a train and crossed the border safely into Poland.

The first and most eminent member of the Alma-Ata community had gotten out. Would the others make it, too?

Reb Yehudah arrived in Moscow, ostensibly on a business trip, while Etta remained in Alma-Ata covering for the family until they could either find some way to get across the border or else give up on the entire idea. Simply leaving the country through normal legal procedures was impossible because of

Reb Yehudah's high profile. When they finally decided to leave, they tried to keep it a secret from everyone, even Millman and Malasha, but it was hard to avoid arousing suspicion. Millman guessed, Malasha guessed, and even the guard dog Silva guessed.

Millman was the first. When the girls were getting ready to travel to Moscow with their grandmother, he came to bid them farewell.

"There is something I would like you to do for me," he requested.

"What?" asked the girls willingly.

"I know you are going to Palestine. When you get there I want you to send a message to a former friend of mine, David Green. Tell him that he was right, that I should have stayed."

"How will he know the message comes from you?" asked the girls, realizing that he was talking about someone important who was not likely to pay much attention to them.

"You can give him a sign. Remind him that at the Zionist Congress I called him a liar. He surely remembers that."

By the time Etta was prepared to leave, Malasha also realized that the family must be planning to flee Russia. She began pleading with Etta to take her, but Etta was adamant in refusing. While the Shkolniks could not lead a safe legal life in Russia, Malasha surely could. It would have been expensive and dangerous to include her, and there was no reason for her to undergo the risks of the journey and the dislocations of leaving her native land. She hoped Malasha's feelings would not be so hurt that she would say something indiscreet.

The night before Etta was to leave Alma-Ata for Moscow, she was awakened by a rasping noise at one of the windows. Silva the watchdog began to bark fiercely, and Etta heard the sound of a shot from the living room. There were more noises she could not identify. She crouched down out of sight behind the bed, feeling intensely the fact that her husband was a five-day journey away. There had been a pained howl from Silva after the shot, so she must have been wounded, but she still barked ferociously. After a while, that was the only noise Etta heard. Cautiously, Etta opened the door from the bedroom to the main room. Silva was standing at the window barking into the darkness; apparently, the intruders had fled. Silva turned her head toward her mistress, and Etta gasped. The shot had destroyed one of Silva's eyes. Etta relatched the shutters, tended Silva's wound and returned to bed. Silva stretched out on a rug near the bed, still on guard.

The following day a wagon pulled up in front of the house. Etta took the Polish passports from their hidingplace and concealed them in her clothing. The items she was planning to take on the journey were brought out and stowed in the back of the wagon. Silva watched all her actions, whining with concern. Etta climbed into the wagon, waving good-bye to Malasha and Silva. The vehicle started moving down the road leading from Tashtag into the train station in Alma-Ata, and Silva trotted after it.

"Go home, Silva," ordered Etta. "Go home!"

Silva would not listen. Even when they reached the outskirts of Alma-Ata proper and the traffic thickened, Silva continued to lope along beside the wagon. Only when they reached the train station, barred to animals, was Silva finally parted from her mistress.

LEMBERG, U.S.S.R.

For an entire month, the Chabad families in Lemberg remained isolated in their hiding places, praying in private and receiving a stipend from the committee to keep them fed and sheltered. The day before *Rosh Hashanah,* each one had individually made the same calculation. All over the world, Jews who never set foot in a *mikveh* all year round were purifying themselves for *Rosh Hashanah.* Could it be that the *chassidim* of Chabad, who were accustomed to go to the *mikveh* every day, would enter the Day of Judgment without a preliminary purification? Separately, each man made his way carefully through the streets to the Lemberg *mikveh.* When he arrived he found it crowded with his fellow *chassidim,* the friends and companions he had not seen for over a month. Together, they took heart and decided to hold prayer services in the apartments on the festival. They prayed fervently for some escape from the trap they were in and hoped that their prayers would be answered.

After the holiday, they began to visit Zev Manevitch in search of some way out. Zev went back to the Polish officials from whom he had bought the unusable passports and pleaded for his companions, describing the conditions of their existence. Finally, he persuaded them to return part of the money he had paid them for the documents. The money was returned to the families according to their means, the poorest families receiving a complete refund.

A rumor spread that men without beards would be able to travel. The committee still judged the dangers of another attempt to be too great. One group of *chassidim,* whose position was particularly desperate, decided on their own to take the risk. They heard that a transport was scheduled to leave for Poland during the Ten Days of Repentance and decided to join it. There were two bearded men in the group, but they had "white beards," generally considered harmless by the government. The elderly people, educated before the revolution, were allowed religious observances. The travellers approaching the train wore a tragic expression on their faces and climbed aboard fearful that they were travelling to death or to prison, and they sat on their bundles saying *Tehillim*. The train carried them to the border, where they had to descend for a person-by-person border check. Each stepped forward when his assumed name was called, not knowing if he was going to Poland or Siberia. Each one stepped forward and was led across the border. They were safe. When the news was sent back to Lemberg and Moscow, everyone took heart.

On the day before *Yom Kippur*, the men assembled at the *mikveh* once more. Once again, they organized small prayer services in various parts of Lemberg to reduce the distance they would have to travel through the streets. For the festival of *Sukkos*, they converted a fence into a *sukkah* so long and narrow that it was inconspicuous, unless one happened to enter the courtyard at a time when thirty bearded men were sitting in a row with their backs to the fence.

After *Sukkos* another desperate group, this time numbering fifty-seven, decided to risk joining the next transport. The group contained nine "black beards," and the risk of arousing suspicion was much greater than with the previous group. Happily, they too got through safely, and then everyone decided to go. The committee was also convinced.

Those *chassidim* who had gotten out immediately contacted the *Rebbe*, Reb Yosef Yitzchak. They described the situation in Lemberg and asked what those left behind in Russia should do. An answer was soon sent to Lemberg saying they should not be afraid to travel, and they received a blessing for success. The *chassidim* began getting their documents in order.

The Shkolniks and the Gershgorens transferred their base to Lemberg. They were to be met in Lemberg by a cousin who was in the army. Like any other group of children on a train ride, Nechamah, Raizel and their cousin Shlomo enjoyed standing at the junction between two cars watching the floor jerk and sway. One of the passengers, who found their family group rather

188 • WINGS ABOVE THE FLAMES

suspicious looking, took the opportunity to interrogate them.

"Where are you going, children?" he asked.

"To Lemberg," answered Nechamah.

"What are you going to do there?"

"We are going to live there," lied Nechamah boldly.

"Who is going to meet you when you get there?"

"My father," asserted Nechamah. "He is an officer in the army."

"Really? Well, I hope you have a nice journey."

Nechamah looked after him as he walked away, not sure whether or not she had succeeded in allaying his suspicions. To bear a secret which could put one's entire family in prison is a heavy responsibility for an eight-year-old girl. Perhaps this man would continue to observe them. She hoped their cousin in Lemberg would not say or do anything to reveal he was not their father.

When they arrived in Lemberg, they found the Chabad community bustling with activity, preparing to send five hundred people on the next transport. Rumor had it that the government officials had changed their minds about the group they had stopped in the summer, and were willing to revalidate those passports, in return for a large bribe.

The money was collected, and a woman named Mrs. Roth was dispatched to bring the money to the office involved. She delivered the cash, declaring it "a present from the knitwear factory." A date in mid-November was fixed when she was to bring the three hundred passports to the office that would validate them, and she would be allowed to add new passports for additional passengers.

The date chosen was a Friday. Mrs. Roth carried the passports for the sixty-eight families, each with a picture of the head of the family. For security, another man accompanied her as far as the door of the office, then stepped back to wait for her outside. As he stood there watchfully, he realized with alarm that they had been followed and that a car was waiting nearby. After a few minutes, Mrs. Roth came out very agitated with the passports still in her hands.

"Quick, take me to Zev Manevitch," she demanded. "I have to speak to him!"

"We're being watched," whispered her companion. "Don't say anything."

The two separated and walked off in different directions. Two men raced after Mrs. Roth, signalling with their hands to someone else. A car pulled up, the men grasped Mrs. Roth, and she was forced into the back seat. Her former escort, after some precautions to shake any pursuers, informed the committee of the ominous developments.

The next morning, a *Shabbos*, Mrs. Roth's brother was arrested. The police also showed up at the Roth's apartment, intending to arrest her husband, but he was not there. They arrested her son, a boy of sixteen, in his place. Another family, having realized that their apartment was under surveillance, fled before policemen arrived to arrest them.

The committee deduced that Mrs. Roth's arrest had been coordinated in advance with the officials at the passport office. They had her transport the documents, so that she would be caught with all the incriminating material on her person. Apparently, the offer to revalidate the passports had been a ruse.

That evening, Mrs. Roth's brother and son were released, bringing more disturbing news. Their captors had shouted at them, "Why do you want to flee from the Soviet Union, and worse, under the guise of Poles? We know your secret, that you aren't planning to stay in Poland but to travel farther. For two transports we looked the other way; we thought that would be the end of the matter. And here, you keep on going. Enough! From now on all the paths are closed to you. We now have a list of all your names, along with sixty-eight pictures."

The committee had already sent messengers to Vilna, Baronovich and other cities, but Lemberg had proven to be the only possibility of escape. Now that was being closed too. The whole Chabad community was tense with fear, as they had been after the warning the previous summer. No one knew when the police might knock at his own door.

The Shkolniks and the Gershgorens had not arranged their documents through the committee and were not on the list which had fallen into the hands of the police. But they did have a reason to fear discovery. The manager who had replaced Reb Yehudah in the knitwear factory in Alma-Ata had embezzled large amounts of money and equipment and laid the blame on Reb Yehudah. By the time Etta had reached Moscow, there was already a police bulletin out for her arrest. The Shkolniks could not return to their old Russian identities, and their new Polish identities would not stand up to close examination, since none of them spoke Polish. The risk of staying in the country seemed as great as the risk of leaving, so they decided on an attempt to leave with the next transports.

The committee, encouraged by the Rebbe's blessing, made a similar decision. They would buy new passports and go, whatever the danger. The risk being so great, they first polled the women to see if they were willing to accept the danger. Their answer was unequivocal. They would go.

A serious problem remained. From where could they get the money for new passports? The going rate was fifteen thousand rubles per person registered on a passport. Passports for a hundred people would alone cost more than a million rubles. The resources of the community had already been strained by the previous purchases and by supporting, so many months, all those people in Lemberg who could not work because they had not registered.

The committee appointed a court of twenty-three judges, which decided that everyone who had gold, dollars, jewelry or gems was required to surrender them as a loan to be repaid on the other side of the border. Anyone who held back would be expelled from the Chabad community, and the merit of the *rebbes* would no longer aid him on the Day of Judgment. The *chassidim* all accepted the decision, turning over enough assets to buy passports for two hundred and forty-four people. Within a week after the arrests, they were ready to travel.

Reb Yehudah, not belonging to the Chabad community, was not bound by the judgment, but in fact he had already paid out all his wealth as loans and donations to people who wanted to buy passports. The Shkolniks had nothing left with which to make a new start within Russia, no money, no connections, not even a usable identity. Everything hung on the outcome of the transport.

The Gershgorens left first. They travelled in freight cars, arriving at the border in the middle of the night. The guards began checking passports. One young man was arrested and led away on the grounds that his passport was forged, which it was. A woman named Pearl was also moved out of the group and left aside while her documents were checked. At some point, when the guards were not looking, she slipped away, climbed back into the train and wormed her way under the mound of baggage at one end of the car.

"Pearl, Pearl! Where is Pearl?" the guards began to shout when they noticed her disappearance. They searched the station, then unloaded everyone from the train and began to rummage about in the luggage. It was late at night, and they were tired. They did not have the energy to unload all the packages and check everything. After a while, they abandoned the search.

At three in the morning, the young man who had been taken away was brought back.

"I'm being arrested," he said to his bride of six months. "They let me come to get my things. I need my *tallis* and *tefillin*."

His bride and her partially paralyzed mother were stricken by the news. What were his chances of getting out of Russia once he was released? The young man's elder brother was worried that he might vanish without a trace, leaving his new wife unable to marry.

"Quick," he urged. "There are two rabbis among the passengers. Let's write out a conditional divorce for your wife, in case you should disappear."

When the bride and her mother heard the word "divorce," they both went into hysterics. The idea had to be abandoned.

The young man, arbitrarily chosen as a victim to prove the efficiency of the Russian border guards, was led away into the dark, and the train continued into Poland, with Pearl still safely concealed under the luggage.

The Shkolniks were scheduled to leave on a transport a week later, departing just after *Shabbos* would end. The travellers assembled in groups according to their putative family make-up. The passports were generally a poor match for their owners. It was possible to add children onto the list of dependents, but naturally, only in descending order of age. Nor could the sex or age of a child already registered be easily changed. Sons were registered as brothers, children as grandchildren, boys as girls. Superfluous children from one family were attached to another family with extra dependents on its list. The entire matching operation had required great talent on the part of the organizing committee, and it had all been done in the space of the few days between the purchase of the passports and departure of the transport. Up until the moment of arrival at the train station, mothers were still rehearsing with their children the children's assumed names and family status.

One widow had a seventeen-year-old son named Shmerl, just beginning to sprout a fluffy little beard. According to the passport she carried, she had a daughter named Basya. Shmerl was dressed up in one of his mother's old dresses, and an enormous Russian wool scarf was wrapped over his head, back around to cover his face, so that the beard would not show. He was a satisfactory looking girl, but his mother had to keep her eye on him to prevent him from making some mistake, like standing up to pray with the fervor of a *yeshivah* boy.

The train was waiting in the station. Since the cost of the transport was being borne by the Soviet government, it had not spared passenger trains for the purpose, but only freight cars. When *Shabbos* was over the men loaded the bundles into the empty cars. The luggage was arrayed along the side of the car, so that the weak and the old could take turns sitting on it. Everyone else would have to stand through the whole journey.

The train moved jerkily toward the border. The passengers would cross through several towns before reaching the border checkpoint where their passports would be scrutinized. One danger, at least, had passed. They had not been arrested at the train station. However, knowing the preference of the MGB for catching people red-handed, any intended arrests were more likely to be made at the border.

It was growing late at night, and Etta was tiring. Behind her was a fur-wrapped bundle, and after a while Etta sat down. Reb Yehudah, standing farther down the car, noticed the disappearance of his wife's head.

"Did you find someplace to sit?" he called out, pleased.

"Oh, yes, I'm very comfortable," answered Etta.

"You may be comfortable, but I'm not," growled a voice from beneath her.

Etta jumped up and whirled around. What she had taken for a bundle of clothing was a bent old man in an enormous fur coat.

Should she admit her error, or should she let him think she had sat on him deliberately? How do you apologize to someone you have mistaken for a piece of luggage? "I didn't realize . . . I'm terribly sorry . . ."

He did not seem mollified by any of her attempts to apologize, and finally, she gave up in embarrassment. If they all got out safely, when he told the story of this train ride, he would probably always add, ". . . and then some woman plunked herself down on my back as if I were a footstool."

If they all got out safely.

In another part of the car, a woman who had been bent over her bundles suddenly began to shriek hysterically.

"It's gone! It's gone! It's been lost!"

"What's lost?" asked her neighbors.

"Describe it. Maybe someone saw it," suggested another.

They would have been happy to help her look for a lost watch or some other valuable item.

"My little son's bedpan is missing! Oh, whatever will I do! *Oy, oy, oy.*"

The people standing around felt that their sympathies had been rather abused.

"Don't make such a fuss. Someone else will loan you hers, and when you get to Cracow, G-d willing, you'll buy a new one."

"No, no, no. He won't use anything but that very one. It was tin and round and had a small handle on one side. Hasn't anyone seen it? Could someone have stolen it?"

She bent down and began pawing desperately through her possessions again, still hoping to find it in one of the bundles. All the while, she continued to wail and deplore her bad fortune. Her neighbors, disgusted by such a scene being made over such an insignificant object, turned away. Etta came forward and bent down as if she too were helping with the search.

"Tell me," she said quietly to the distraught woman. "Did it have a false bottom?"

The woman glanced up with gratitude that someone understood the seriousness of her loss.

"Gold?" asked Etta.

The mother nodded.

She helped the woman search, but neither of them found anything.

Late in the night, the train reached the border. The passengers all disembarked, carrying their bundles with them. They were to cross into Poland on foot. It had been cold in the poorly-sealed freight cars, but it was yet colder standing on the snowy ground, exposed to a chilly night wind. One baby was crying bitterly, and the small children, roused from their sleep on the piles of bundles, were whimpering.

The adults were tense with fear of discovery, and the procedure of disembarking itself was nerve-wracking. The official at the gate held a list of repatriates who had been approved for this transport. He would call out the name of a family, and the group of people travelling under that assumed name would straggle forward with all their bundles. The official would check off each individual on the family passport as they passed through the gate on the Russian side and crossed over to the gate on the Polish side.

"Weinberg!"

The "Weinbergs" came forward. Each gave his assumed name.

"Shlomo."

"Risha."

"Chanah."

"David."

"Frieda."

"Yaakov."

"Kagan!" The widow walked over to the gate, with her son Shmerl trailing behind. Those who knew that this "girl" had a beard under her scarf watched covertly to see if the costume would pass inspection. If Shmerl was unmasked, everyone coming after would probably be subjected to much closer inspection, and Shmerl himself would be in terrible trouble.

"Bluma," announced the widow. She started to walk through the gate, and Shmerl followed after her, without saying a word.

"You, girl, stop. What is your name?"

Shmerl stopped in place, but gave no answer. With leaden hearts, the other passengers realized that he had forgotten his feminine first name.

"What is your name?" shouted the irritated official, stepping closer to the supposed girl. Shmerl's two frightened eyes stared out between successive turns of the scarf. Should he run away? Should he confess? Should he pretend to be deaf? Should he simply pray?

The widow was not going to leave everyone's fate in the hands of her bewildered son. She stepped forward, lifted her hand above her shoulder and delivered a hard slap to his wool-wrapped cheek.

"Basya!" she screamed. "Why don't you answer the man!"

"Basya," declared Shmerl in the artificially high-pitched voice his mother had trained him to use. "My name is Basya."

The official, his irritation somewhat relieved by seeing the mother's blow, checked off the name and allowed the pair to pass through the gate.

At last the Shkolniks themselves were called. "Stavitsky!"

"Naftali."

"Rivkah."

"Rachel."

"Bluma."

The four of them walked across the snow to the other gate.

The adventure was far from over, but the most dangerous point had passed.

The families reloaded their possessions in the train. The baby was still crying, and his young mother was advised to wrap him well against the cold and was given a place to sit. The child, completely encased in the folds of a large scarf, began to quiet down. As the train jerked forward, the mother rocked him gently until she too began to doze. This was the only child she had to attend to.

A hush fell over the car. The children were asleep on the packages, and the adults napped on their feet. Some time passed this way in quiet, then everyone was shaken out of their stupor by a new set of shrieks, coming from the mother of the baby. Several experienced mothers hurried over to see what was wrong.

"My baby! My baby! It isn't moving!"

One of the women took the bundle of wool out of his mother's arms and unwrapped it. The child's face was tinged with blue. It was clear at once that he was dead, probably from suffocation, but no one wanted to tell the mother she had smothered her own baby in her efforts to warm him. They simply announced that he had died, maintaining a tactful silence about the cause of the tragedy.

The father was afraid that if they brought the child's body into Cracow, they would become involved in bureaucratic tangles best avoided by non-Polish speakers travelling on Polish identity papers. He enlisted another Jew from the transport to help him. The two of them got off the train in a small village, the father carrying the child's still body. They would try to locate a Jewish cemetery, and if they could not find one, they would bury the child's body in the woods. The mother, sobbing pitifully, continued on with the other passengers to Cracow.

When the transport reached the Cracow train station, the

group was met by representatives of Brichah, an underground organization that helped move Jews across closed borders. The families, stiff with cold and worn down by hours of jostling in the crowded train, climbed out of the cars and lowered their baggage to the platform. The Brichah agents loaded them into trucks before they would attract unwelcome attention from the Polish police. The bereaved mother, her face swollen from crying, was helped down from the wagon and led to the waiting trucks.

The refugees were housed in the auditorium of an abandoned school. The most welcome discovery which awaited them in their new quarters was a stove in one wall. They filled it with available scrap wood, lit a fire and gathered as close around it as possible. A pillar of smoke climbed up the chimney, but then curled around and came back out into the auditorium. Within ten minutes the accumulated smoke, building up in a layer below the ceiling, had descended to the point that the refugees were beginning to cough and choke.

"Put it out! We'll all suffocate!"

Hacking and sneezing was heard from all sides. Reluctantly, the fire-tenders, who had been close enough to really enjoy the warmth, put out the flames. When the stove was sufficiently cool to touch, they poked ineffectually at the obstruction in the chimney, but it soon became clear that years of birds' nests had been built in the narrow mouth since the stove was last used. Everyone would just have to remain cold.

They sat there on the floor, cold, tired and frightened, for three weeks. Everyone, particularly every bearded man, was afraid to go out into the streets without any knowledge of Polish. Brichah did provide them with kosher food, but was not particularly sympathetic to the problems of religious Jews.

The waiting ended with another convoy of trucks carrying them back to the railroad station. This time they were aiming for the German border, which they were going to cross on foot. They descended from the train.

Their guides led them in a straggling line through fields and woods. The children were hushed into silence, and the fear of the parents was so obvious that the children found it easy to be still. As their group drew near the border, the Brichah leader, a rifle slung across his shoulder, sent word down the line that a sentry was passing and that no noise of any kind was allowed. When the guard was safely past and out of earshot, the guide cut a hole in the barbed wire of the border fence and began moving people through as quickly as possible. He, too, was afraid. It showed on his face and in the tenseness of his voice.

"Hurry through, will you? Hurry! Anyone who holds us all up is going to be shot."

Indeed, he and his friend had their guns pointing at their charges as they tried to combat the frightened and hesitant refugees afraid to go through the fence and cross the open space beyond. Finally, one balky refugee so upset the guide that his nerves snapped and he killed the man. There were no more delays on the part of the fugitives, but now they were as afraid of their rescuers as of the border police.

They continued their journey through Czechoslovakia to Austria. On *Shabbos Chanukah*, their trucks arrived in Vienna, in the American Occupation Zone.

"Unload your things," shouted the guide.

"We can't," answered the refugees. "Today is *Shabbos*."

"If you won't unload it," growled the man, with assorted insults, "then you will have to put up with the way *we* unload it."

The Brichah agents began tossing the bundles carelessly over the sides of the trucks, with no concern about breakage. The refugees sat down stoically to wait for *Shabbos* to end so that they could reassemble their things. What did it matter, really, that their possessions were damaged? They themselves had arrived intact in the American Occupation Zone. The danger of being returned to Russia had ended.

EPILOGUE

R ebbetzin Chanah arrived safely in Paris, where she was reunited with her son after a separation of eighteen years. They then moved to the United States. Rav Menachem Mendel *shlita* inherited the leadership of the Chabad *chassidim* from his father-in-law, and Rebbetzin Chanah lived near him in Brooklyn, witnessing his efforts on behalf of Judaism in Russia and other scattered parts of the world. She left behind a book of memoirs.

True to their principles, the men of the Lemberg committee did not attempt to leave Russia until all the transports had gone. Tragically, they were arrested by the MGB when their regular passenger train stopped at the border. Upon hearing news of the arrests, others among the organizers in Lemberg took cover. *Die Muma Sarah* came there to help maintain the Chabad families still stranded there, until at last they dispersed.

In 1950, the MGB reopened the case and arrested many of the Jews involved in the Lemberg operation, including *die Muma Sarah* and her son. She refused to incriminate anyone else. They confronted her with her son, to prove he was under their power. She gave him a few cubes of sugar she had been saving for sustenance on *Pesach*, saying that she would not be needing them. They put her son in a neighboring room and threatened to torture him if she would not talk. *Die Muma* Sarah collapsed from a heart attack and returned her soul to her Creator in sanctification of G-d's name.

Rebbetzin Leah and the rest of her family, including the Shkolniks, lived first in a refugee camp in Wegsheid, Austria, and afterwards in an apartment building in Paris rented by the Joint Distribution Committee to house Jewish refugees. In 1948, when immigration to Israel had become possible, they all joined her son who had moved there ten years earlier and was serving as the rabbi of a settlement. Reb Yehudah's fortune was never returned, but starting from scratch, he founded a factory. Etta became a teacher and eventually founded a home for orphaned immigrant children. The Shkolniks had grandsons who eventually numbered among the top students of Ponevezh Yeshivah. Millman's message was delivered to David Ben-Gurion.

A religious emigrant from Moscow commented once that he had never found, in the outside world, quite the intensity of holiness of a *Simchas Torah* in Russia. When it is black outside, he claimed, you fully feel the light in the little corner of holiness you create for yourself. Nechamah Shkolnik, having spent her early years in such a bright corner, had an answer ready.

"Yes," she said. "But there are so very few of those corners in Russia."

In the explosive clash of forest fire and glacier, some of the seeds, carried in updrafts from the flames, come to rest far up the glacier. Snow falls and freezes, and the seed is trapped in the ice, not to be freed until the ice would thaw.

BURIED IN SNOW 6

T he Transylvanian town of Satmar, where Asher Nadel lived, was noted for the scholarship of its *rav*, the piety of its Jews and the poverty of its inhabitants. One would hardly believe that the anti-Semitism and the poverty could grow much worse, but with the outbreak of war, they did.

Transylvania was a border area under continual dispute between Romania and Hungary, and the inhabitants therefore spoke both languages. Between the wars it was in Romanian control, but late in 1940 the Germans ceded it to Hungary. Immediately, at age twenty, Asher was drafted to the Hungarian military, given a gun and taught to shoot. When Asher had been a soldier in basic training for four weeks, the Hungarians took away all Jews' guns and uniforms and gave them spades and work clothes instead. After spending a few weeks in bunkers along the Slovakian border with nothing much to do, Asher and his fellow Transylvanian draftees were sent to Budapest.

Early in 1941, though Hungary was not yet in the war, she was preparing for it vigorously. An area outside Budapest which had held country homes for the wealthy was made over into a large army camp for repairing trucks, tanks and other machinery. In order to make an impressive entrance, the army decided to landscape a park between the main gate and the building, so they called in Jewish labor battalions and set them to work. Some Jews were sent to the fields to cut blocks of sod, some transported them, and some, including Asher, were assigned to lay them in place, a relatively easy job. They had an enormous area to cover, and the project took months. It was not what Asher had been expecting when he was first drafted, but things could have been worse.

When Germany invaded Russia, and Hungary joined the war in the hope of gaining spoils, things did get worse. Much worse. The Jewish labor battalions were sent in to build roads, and the moment they arrived in the Ukraine, they had vivid proof that life was about to be very different from one of landscaping an army base. The roads down which they drove were lined on each side with a row of trees, and in each tree hung corpses of murdered men.

Asher and his fellow Transylvanians were joined together in the Ukraine with a group of Hungarian Jews, and bedded down in the barn of a *kolkhoz*, a collective farm. There were no men left in the area. Those who had been there had been killed, had escaped with the Russians or had joined the partisans. Most of the battalion was set to work digging ditches along the road-beds for drainage. Asher's luck held, and he got the relatively easy job of chopping wood for the kitchen fires.

While they were in the forest chopping wood, they would be approached by Ukrainian peasant women offering to exchange potatoes for ready-cut sticks of wood for their ovens. The Jewish laborers made this trade a regular way of supplementing the meager rations of their comrades. They would build a fire in the late afternoon and roast the potatoes in the embers. Then they would bring them back to the barn, where they would be waiting, still hot to the touch and warming to the stomach, when the road crews returned from their arduous assignment.

The battalion of one hundred and fifty Jews was divided into three brigades of fifty, each with a brigade leader and a complement of Hungarian soldiers. The leader of one brigade expected to bring his Jews home with him alive at the end of the war. The leader of another one was rather indifferent to his men's fate. The leader of the third, the commander of Asher's brigade, told them straight out, "I don't expect to leave here until every single Jew is dead."

The commander was a Schwabian, an ethnic German notorious for anti-Semitism. However, his hatred for the Jews in his brigade had a personal element as well, for the Hungarian Jews among them came from the same town, Petsh, as he and his men. Unlike the Transylvanian Jews, the Hungarian Jews were university educated, sons of well-to-do, middle-class parents, and they were unused to performing miscellaneous work on demand.

Every morning, the ditch-diggers were sent out to work on the roads, each worker being assigned to dig a ten-meter stretch. The Hungarian Jews, being more accustomed to work with a pencil than with a spade, never made their quota. The commander began with punishments. Toward the end of the day, the foreman would go around, pull out all the workers who had fallen behind in their work, bind them hand and foot and leave them lying helpless in the bitter cold at the side of the road until the end of the shift. After being released and marched back to camp, their hands would be bound again, and the "delinquents" would be strung up in a row. If one of them fainted, the guards would take him down, pour water over him until he revived and then string him up again. The Hungarian boys, broken by the grueling torture, began to die one by one. Inspectors from the headquarters a few towns away asked the commander why so many more were dying in his brigade than in others, but he gave no explanation.

A Jewish boy named Schnitzer escaped from their camp and made his way by foot to the headquarters, where he reported the commander's methods. Instead of gaining sympathy, however, he was returned to the camp and to the tortures of the Schwabian, who soon succeeded in killing him. Later, the boy's father pleaded, "If you won't send me back my boy alive, at least send me his ashes." But even that was denied him.

Asher's battalion had been in the Ukraine for over a year when the Russian counter-offensive broke through the German lines at Stalingrad and the German army began its retreat through the winter snow. The soldiers withdrew first, and the labor battalions were left in wagons in the rear. For the first time in two years, Asher was again handed a rifle and told to act like a soldier. So they want me to guard them, thought Asher with scorn. In defiance, at the first opportunity, he and some of his friends hurled their rifles into a snowbank, dropped off the wagons and headed across the fields, hoping to hide out until the Russians would arrive.

Although night had fallen, the sky over Asher and his fellow deserters was lit up by the Russian artillery bursts. They desperately wanted shelter from the cold and from the dangers of the battlefront. The best they could find was a snow-covered haystack, so they tunnelled in and tried to settle down for the night. They were not left alone in their refuge for long. Soldiers of all the Axis nationalities, fleeing from the advancing Red Army, tunnelled in to join them—Germans, Hungarians, Italians. In the middle of the night, there was a change in the sounds; instead of the blasts of the artillery, they heard the whiz of rifle bullets. The infantry must be closing in. The soldiers abandoned the haystack and fled; the Jews kept their places. They were awaiting liberation, not fleeing capture.

When dawn broke, a few went out to reconnoiter. The Axis troops were gone, and the roadsides were littered with food they had thrown off trucks and wagons in order to flee faster. Overjoyed and ravenous, the reconnoiterers brought their whole group to the spot, where they gathered bags of flour and other foodstuffs and took them into an abandoned dwelling with a brick oven.

Asher and his companions decided to celebrate with a feast and set about making bread and cooking a stew. They made a pact not to pre-taste anything at all; they would all eat together at the meal. Waiting was part of the pleasure; it would make the feast that much more delightful. The bread was almost baked and the stew filled the room with a delicious aroma, when they suddenly heard the rumble of vehicles outside. A Russian officer appeared in the doorway, presumably drawn by the smoke rising from the chimney. One of them quickly explained that they were not enemy soldiers, but rather Jews who had been pressed into forced labor. From the hard expression on the officer's face they saw this explanation was not well-received. He made them line up, and his men searched them one by one, taking every object of any value, and even pieces of clothing. Asher was left with only his mess kit and a single beet.

"Outside!" the Russian barked.

"But our food!" protested one of them. "We haven't eaten anything for a day."

"You can leave the food for the landlady," said the officer with a disdainful laugh.

"There is no landlady. The house is deserted."

"That's what you think. Babushka!" he called. "Come out."

A Ukrainian peasant woman with her two children came out

hesitantly from a bunker in the yard where she had been hiding.

"Our prisoners did you a favor," the officer said. "They cooked your meal for you."

She bobbed her head in appreciation and scurried into the house, closing the door after herself.

The Jews were led off and herded in with a group of captured Axis soldiers, who glowered at them menacingly. There was no evidence of any intention to feed the prisoners. The men in Asher's group were exhausted, famished and frightened. This was hardly the liberation of which they had dreamed.

In all the comings and goings, Asher spotted an officer who looked Jewish. Asher waited until he came close and then whispered in Yiddish, "Do we Jews really have to be kept in with these murderers?"

The officer looked them over coolly, then glanced at the Axis soldiers.

"All right," he said. "I'll let you go to Davidovka, where the prisoners are being concentrated." He wrote out a pass for the group of Jews.

"Can we have provisions for the journey?" one of them asked hopefully.

"A way down the road there's an army camp," he said. "Report there, and they will give you something."

Still uninitiated in the Soviet system, they naively believed him. They hiked down the road to the army camp, displayed their pass and asked for food.

"Not here," they were told. "At the next camp down."

There they also met with disappointment.

"I don't see any way out of this," said one of them. "I think we'll have to beg."

They split up and knocked on doors along the road, one or two at a time. In each house, the peasants were cooking the same stew, made of potatoes, beans, dried peas and a little rice, called *borscht.* The peasants obligingly ladled a little into the men's tin mess plates. Both the warmth and the nourishment were very welcome after a day of privation.

After their disappointment of the morning, things seemed to be looking up. For one thing, they were no longer serving under Nazis. And though still prisoners of the Russians, they had been released on their own responsibility, a privilege the Germans would never have gotten. And now they were no longer starving, and the exercise kept them from freezing. The eternal optimism of the Jew left them totally unprepared for the calamitous tragedy about to befall them.

As they came to a deserted stretch of road that began to pass open fields, a single tank rumbled toward them. On guard, in the turret, stood a short, wiry soldier holding a submachine gun, his torso completely draped in loops of ammunition. As the tank approached, they saw he was a Mongol, with hardly any nose at all. He looked so savage that they pulled out their pass for presentation, expecting him to challenge them.

The tank drew abreast of them, and the Mongol barked out some order which halted it. Ignoring their pass, which he quite possibly could not read anyway, he gestured for them to lie down in a row at the side of the road. They complied. He raised his gun and fired a round of bullets which raked the row of men from one end to the other. There was a moment of silence, then one by one he fired spurts of bullets at those Jews who were crying out or writhing in pain. The firing did not stop until all the Jews were lying still and motionless on the turf. The vulgar Mongol gave another call to the crew of the tank, and it rumbled on its way until it was finally out of earshot.

Only a few of the Jews had survived, those who had realized in a flash, during the first volley, that they must control themselves and not move, no matter how painful their wounds. Asher was one of the few. He had been wounded in the legs, but not seriously enough to be kept from walking. No one escaped unwounded, and they could not bury their fallen comrades. Not only was the ground frozen solid, even the snow was crusted over, and they had nothing with which to dig.

It was a very bedraggled group which finally staggered into Davidovka that evening. The prisoners of war were concentrated in the old part of town in primitive sod houses. The available houses were already so crowded that it was impossible to find room even for their small group. Eventually, they located a cellar and slid down the mud to take shelter. At least the roof kept off the rain and the walls provided shelter from the wind. There they spent a miserable night, nursing their wounds. In the morning, they received no breakfast, not belonging to any of the houses to which food was being distributed.

They renewed the search for drier accommodations. One of them noticed a group of Russian guards, carrying all their equipment, leaving one of the houses.

"Quick, let's take their place before any others do!"

They scurried in and took the places of the men who had just left.

With so many men crowded into so little space with no opportunity to bathe or wash clothes, lice-borne typhus spread with devastating swiftness. Although no one died the first night, those who awoke the morning after the second night found themselves in the company of several corpses. By the third night, there were yet more. Asher decided that if he wanted to survive, he would have to get out of this plague area.

As a prisoner, he could not just go. The only people who got out of his compound were those who carried the sick to the nearest field hospital. But if that was what was required, that was what he would do. Asher picked up one of the sick men, slung him over his back and set out for the hospital.

The hospital was a horrendous sight. The sick men lay on

straw on the floor, one next to the other, the dead next to the living, with no improvement in cleanliness over the houses he had just left.

One of the harried doctors glanced at the man Asher was carrying and said, "We cannot do anything for him here. Take him back."

Asher had no intention of doing any such thing. He deposited the man in one of the rows of sick people and went outside to look for the kitchen. He found two men working with a large two-man saw, sawing down trees to supply the kitchen with firewood. As he approached, one of the pair, clutched his stomach and vanished into the woods.

"Shall I take his place in the meantime?" volunteered Asher.

"Sure," said the other fellow. "I'm not even sure he's coming back. He was weak already, and that kind of diarrhea is a murderer."

Indeed, Asher sawed for the rest of the shift, and the other worker never reappeared. After a while, the cook appeared to see how they were doing and brought them bread to eat. Asher ate a little bit but set the rest aside, afraid that he, too, would come down with diarrhea if he ate too much after starving so long.

"I see you have a lot of sense," said the cook approvingly. "When you finish this job, come help me in the kitchen."

Asher reported to his new job.

"All right," said the cook. "You can start by stirring this pot."

Asher's clothes were not only swarming with lice, they were piled with lice. The first thing he did that night was wash and fumigate his clothes in a hot oven. Then he took stock of his new situation. He had food, warmth and shelter. He could get along with his employer. Still, the danger of contracting typhus was ever-present.

Asher decided to move into the interior of Russia in search of safer quarters. There was a fellow who delivered bread every day, and Asher asked him to note when a train arrived to move prisoners into Russia. In the meantime, he had not yet come down with typhus, and at least he was getting regular meals.

One day, the man who brought the bread reported that a train was at the station, being filled up with prisoners of war. Asher turned to the cook and handed over the spoon with which he was stirring.

"Here, you'll have to take over," Asher asserted.

The cook looked nonplussed but had little choice. He took the spoon and began to stir.

Asher took a short cut through the fields. He could see the train waiting on the track, but had no idea how long it would remain there. A Russian soldier accosted him on the way, pushed him down and tried to steal his boots. When the Russian had wrenched one off, Asher sprang to his feet and sprinted away through the snow, with one foot bare.

He arrived at the train just in time and climbed into one of the wagons. Looking around, he found an acquaintance from back home by the name of Mendel Greenbaum.

"Do you know where we are going?" Asher asked.

"No," Mendel replied. "But, I hope it is to a better place than this."

They quickly discovered that they might not survive the journey long enough to realize their destination. More than a day passed and no water at all was given to the prisoners. They were weak and fainting when the door was finally opened and someone unceremoniously dumped in a vat of salted herrings, a tempting dish but poison to anyone in these people's condition. Some of the men fell on these and consumed them. Asher and Mendel had more self-restraint. It began to look as if their captors had decided to finish them all off on the journey.

Soon, Asher gained a new pair of boots, as the men in the car began to die of thirst and typhus. Those who had eaten the herrings were among the first to go, their insides burned out by the salt. Now, at every station, the door would open and someone would ask, *"Kaput?"* The men in the wagon would throw out the corpses. No one offered them water.

Their wagon, however, had one major advantage over other wagons in the train. In a corner, lay a thick, sharp nail. The prisoners used it to make a circular groove at one spot in the floor, and from then on they took turns, one after the other, scraping the nail around and around in the gradually deepening groove. Finally, the groove grew so deep that a few hard blows knocked down the circular piece of wood, leaving a small hole in the floor.

They tied a string to one of their canteens, lowered it through the hole and let it bump and bounce for a few minutes on the snow covering the tracks. When they hauled it up they found to their delight that it had gathered a little snow. One of them would eagerly drink the precious moisture and give the canteen to someone else, who would lower it through the hole and repeat the process. Thus they passed their days, fishing continuously for snow.

NIZHNITAGIL, SIBERIA

After several days without food, the entire transport halted at a delousing station. Those who had survived this far were sent to a bathhouse. The prisoners from the other wagons had their first chance to drink and were then dispatched into the interior, still without provisions. Perhaps it was deliberate policy to kill off the prisoners-of-war, or perhaps no one along the way saw feeding these enemy soldiers as his responsibility.

Regardless, the prisoners travelled a total of four weeks with no sustenance but the water they fished up through the hole in the floor of their car.

The transport finally halted at a huge prison complex in the Ural mountain range of Siberia, near the town of Nizhnitagil. After the German invasion most heavy industry had been moved to Siberia. Iron ore mined from the mountains was processed in enormous industrial complexes built by prisoners and equipped with American machines. The entire process took place on the spot, with the iron ore entering one end of the machines and finished tanks rolling out the other.

The newly arrived prisoners were sent to dugout barracks. Asher and Mendel were crammed in with a group of Italian soldiers. When a vat of soup was delivered to the barracks, the Italians scrambled for it, knocked it over, spilled it out, threw themselves down on top of it and began slurping it off the floor. Asher and Mendel stood aghast, wondering when they would ever get something to eat and fearing for their lives among such a pack of animals.

Their barracks was ignored for two days, but the following morning they were called to line up outside for labor assignments. Asher had "inherited" a warm, fur-lined coat from one of the prisoners who had died in transit. He stood shivering inside the coat, awaiting his turn. When the officer reached Asher, he glanced at his emaciated, shivering form and said, "Back inside! You are not fit for work."

This was a catastrophe. Asher had learned from prison scuttlebutt that heavy workers received reasonable rations of bread, while non-workers got only two hundred grams. Asher walked back to the barracks, shed his coat and sped back to the line as if he were someone else arriving late. The ruse worked. He and Mendel were assigned to the corpse detail at the hospital.

When they arrived at the hospital, their first assignment was to carry a dead German soldier from the hospital to the hut which served as a morgue. They dropped him unceremoniously, annoyed at having to perform such a service for an arch-enemy. As they were making another trip, again with a German soldier, two German prisoners-of-war carrying their food ration approached, guarded by a Russian soldier who appeared from his face to be Jewish. As Asher passed by, he whispered to the Russian guard in Yiddish, "Why do we have to carry *this*, while *they*," indicating the Germans and the vat of food, "get to carry *that*?"

The Jew, for so he was, hesitated a moment and then said, "You're right. Switch."

Asher and Mendel happily carried the food into the hospital, while the German prisoners-of-war dragged their dead comrade off to the morgue.

Rations were delivered to the hospital according to the number of sick who were registered, and since many died each day and others could not eat, there was always leftover food. Asher and Mendel thought of their fellow Jews back in the barracks, deprived every day of their soup ration by the rapacious Italian prisoners. They bided their time until they were familiar with the conditions in the kitchen and the hospital and had earned the confidence of the cooks by granting various small favors. Then they set up a soup kitchen for Jewish prisoners.

The location was a small hut in the back of the hospital. They borrowed a number of bread loaf pans from the cooks and spread the word quietly among the Jewish prisoners-of-war that they should come to the hut at a certain time. There, from the unused hospital rations, each one was given a hunk of bread and a loaf pan full of soup.

Once the threat of starvation was removed from themselves and their comrades, Asher and Mendel looked around for some way to further alleviate their own lot. They decided to go into tailoring. The needles were fashioned from pierced wire, the threads were extracted from the lining of a coat, and a razor blade served the place of scissors. The customers had to provide the clothing material, but with the high mortality rate in the camp it was not difficult to inherit clothing. Their first customers were the cooks in the kitchen, who were "well-to-do" relative to other prisoners because of their control of the food supplies, and could pay for tailoring services in food. Asher and Mendel sewed a pair of trousers for each of the cooks.

One day, the commander of the base noticed that all the cooks' trousers were of much better quality than anything the camp provided and started an investigation. The cooks fingered Asher and Mendel as the ones who had provided them with the clothing. They were called in to give an explanation.

They displayed the tools of their trade and discovered that the commander was not interested in curtailing their business but rather in expanding it. They were relieved of kitchen duties, assigned a small work-room, given the sewing machines they requested and set to work sewing clothes for the officers of the camp and their families.

In due time, the general in command of the city of Nizhnitagil noticed that the officers in this particular prison camp were better clothed than those in other camps, and he started an investigation of his own. The commander of the camp tried to squirm out of giving an explanation, but in the end, the city commander found out what he wanted to know and was brought to see Asher's and Mendel's "factory."

It turned out that he had been called to Moscow and needed a general's uniform, with inset stripes going down the sleeves and pants. Asher decided that a great deal had just been revealed about the state of the country, if this officer did not think he would be able to buy a uniform in Moscow. They made the uniform to order, much to the general's satisfaction, and from that time on he was one of their steady "customers."

Eventually, the general forced the camp commander, very unwillingly, to have the entire enterprise moved into the town. Asher and Mendel agreed on the condition they could have more equipment and workers. A mechanical genius among the Jewish prisoners figured out a way to drive fourteen sewing machines with one motor and a long shaft. Their factory employed seventy-five people, all Jewish prisoners from the camp. The camp kept track of the number of prisoners in the factory and the number in the camp at any given time, but they did not keep track of the names, so Asher would not set foot inside the prison camp for six months at a time.

In Russia, it was always necessary to have a little something going on the side to earn extra money, and Asher and Mendel's thing was the manufacturing of women's coats. To promote their talent, they took advantage of the American donation of blankets to the local civilian population. Asher and Mendel took one customer's blanket and made it into an elegant overcoat for her. That was all the advertisement they needed. Every woman in Nizhnitagil wanted her blanket made into a coat as well. They made the coats after hours, at the rate of one per night.

They had regular prayer services in the factory, morning and evening. The NKVD offices were in their building, and one of the police officers was Jewish. When he had a memorial *Kaddish* to recite for either of his parents he would come and join them.

They were constantly on the lookout to help fellow Jews. One of the women living in the same building looked Jewish. To make sure, as she walked past them bringing water one day, they started singing in Yiddish. It seemed to them that she reacted. When they had repeated this maneuver three times they were convinced. Asher and a friend went to the bakery in wide, baggy pants and got bread, four loaves apiece, which they concealed in their trousers. They then paid this woman a visit and offered her the bread. She was overwhelmed with gratitude and told them her story.

She had been evacuated with her small daughter to Siberia at the time of the German invasion, her husband having been kept behind because he was needed in the electric company. They lived in great poverty. Then, one day, she ran into her husband in the street. He had been evacuated at the last moment, to the same town as she, and they had been living within a few kilometers of each other without knowing it for months. From that time on, Asher and his friends did what they could to make the family's life easier.

Whenever the prisoners asked when they would be released, they were told, "When the war is over." So, they waited for the war to be over, each wondering what had become of his family.

Early in 1945, Asher heard the first piece of solid news. Russia had been slowly conquering Hungary through the fall. A Gentile prisoner-of-war whom Asher had known from Satmar arrived in the camp and related that all the Jews of Satmar had been carried away in transports during the early summer.

One day, a friend working inside the camp spotted a post-card addressed to Asher in a pile of prisoners' mail. He took it out of the pile and had it delivered to Asher at the factory. Pasted on the card were pictures of four of Asher's siblings. The message said that they were the only members of his family who had survived Auschwitz and the labor camps long enough to be liberated by the Allied forces. Tearfully, Asher mourned the others, and he framed this picture as a keepsake. Unfortunately, he was certain that any written reply would not be delivered.

In May, 1945, the war in Europe ended. Now Asher and his friends began agitating in earnest for their release. However, the Soviets, intent on consolidating their conquests in Eastern

Europe, were in no hurry to close down the tank and armaments factories in Siberia, which ran on prisoner-of-war labor. The only prisoners they sent home were those too weak to work.

Many of the prisoners took advantage of this one loophole. They surreptitiously starved themselves for a month until they were unfit for labor, and thus they obtained their release. They were not allowed to take anything out with them. At the checkpoint for leaving the prison complex, they had to leave all their clothes and belongings, being given new clothes on the other side.

A Gentile from Satmar was one of those who used the starvation route. Asher enlisted his help to try to send a message to his siblings. On a very small piece of paper, he wrote that they should not wait for him to be released but should try to get out of Europe and go to the Land of Israel. He folded the paper into a very small square, the Gentile put it in his ear, and then they plugged both his ears with cotton wool. The ruse fooled the border guards, and the message got through.

Having achieved such respectable positions through their enterprises, Asher and his friends felt that the starvation route was beneath them. Instead, they staged a formal hunger strike. According to regulations, this would have to be reported after three days to the central administration, something the local authorities would prefer to avoid. Their Jewish NKVD man came to negotiate with them.

"You always told us," the two hunger strikers complained, "that at the end of the war we would go home. The war is over!"

"These things are never managed in a minute," said the NKVD man.

"You let plenty of other prisoners go," replied the pair. "Germans, Italians, Hungarians, Poles ... Why do the Jews have to keep slaving away?"

"I will tell you what," said the officer. "You call off this hunger strike, and I give you my word of honor you will be on the next transport that goes out."

Asher and his friends reluctantly agreed. What other guarantee could they expect? But after a few days, a transport went out without them on it.

The next time the NKVD man appeared in their shop, they spit in his face.

"That's what your word of honor is worth!" they hissed.

"I could shoot you all for that sort of insubordination," the officer blustered furiously.

But they knew him too well to think he would really do it.

Wheedling, going on strike, talking back, nothing helped. The Jews remained in Siberia for three more long years, running their factory. They had made themselves too indispensable.

When they were finally released, they were at least sent away with honor. By order of the city commander, as a sign of appreciation, each of the Jews was given a suitcase and new clothing. When they got to the border, instead of being stripped, they were allowed to walk through fully clothed, with their suitcases untouched.

Asher settled in the Land of Israel, where he was reunited with his siblings. He married a new immigrant from Romania named Sarah, whose town had been liberated by the Russians just half an hour before they had been told to assemble for what they believed was to be a mass execution.

Sarah had not immigrated to Israel immediately. Although the Russians allowed many Jews, including Sarah's parents and family, to emigrate during the first years after the war, she had inexplicably been denied a visa every time she applied. Finally, she went to the Bochiver Rebbe in Bucharest for advice. He told her to wait outside the office of the parliament in the morning, to approach a woman who would arrive at a certain time and to request, weeping, that she be allowed to speak to Ana Parker, the Jewish Foreign Minister. She followed the *rebbe's* instruction in every detail. It was not difficult to cry as she made her request.

The woman was Ana Parker's private secretary. She took pity on Sarah and arranged an audience for her with the Foreign Minister herself, who told her to resubmit her visa application.

"I've already submitted it many times!" wailed Sarah.

"Yes," said Ana Parker. "But this time it will go through." So it did.

Asher opened a prosperous dry cleaning business. Although he is by now past retirement age, he keeps the business going full scale, for he has four orphaned grandchildren to marry off. Instead of seventy workers, he now has one, but he is content. He pays his worker every night for the day's work and has not missed once in the twenty-five years that the man has been working for him. Asher explains, "This much I learned from my father, and I have always stuck to it. A worker should be paid on time."

Perhaps some of Asher's success as a factory manager in Siberia was due to the Jewish business ethics he learned from his father.

One winged seed flutters along, almost grazing the flames. It grows scorched and battered, until its wings can barely hold it aloft. But the forest fire is also burning itself out. Which would sink faster, the tattered seed or the flickering flames? Suddenly, a burst of thunder heralds the rainstorm which would extinguish what remained of the fire. The whistling winds rise to gale force, sweep up the faltering seed, and lift it high above the smoldering embers of the fire. On and on it is carried, over blackened earth and scorched tree stumps, toward the mountains in the East.

The wind smacks into a towering wall of ice. With a shriek of protest, it climbs up and over the enormous glacier's lip. The seed is left behind, caught in a crevice of the icy barrier. Not every seed which survives a fire has the good fortune to land in a fertile plot of soil.

BATTERED BY THE STORM | 7

C ecelia Adler was proud of her brother Yitzchak. She herself, as a girl of fourteen, had carried him on a pillow to his circumcision. Twenty-five years had passed since that day. Cecelia herself never married, so she was at home to watch him as he grew into a fine-looking *yeshivah* boy and then set out to study in the court of the Rebbe of Munkacs, one of the Torah giants of Hungary. He so distinguished himself there that he was chosen to edit the *rebbe's* commentaries on the Jerusalem Talmud, after the *rebbe* passed away.

Yitzchak worked in the Adler's courtyard, which contained a little summer house with a conical roof; Yitzchak would sit bent over the manuscript at a little table, his earlocks gently swaying as he made his own neat, corrected copy for the printer. Cecelia, working in the garden, would watch in pleasure as he labored at his project.

Some time after finishing the project, Yitzchak became

engaged. The wedding was held in the summer of 1943. It was a large one. Besides Cecelia and a younger unmarried son, the Adlers had six more grown children, all with families of their own; some already had five or six children. Adding on both sides' cousins, neighbors and family friends, the guests were quite numerous. Yitzchak and his bride moved into their new home, a small room in a different part of town.

When the Germans took over Hungary, and the Jews from the small towns were moved to the cities, Cecelia's home filled up with aunts, uncles and cousins from the provinces. Unlike Yitzchak's wedding a few short months earlier, this family reunion was a much grimmer occasion

After *Pesach*, the transports began. Two thousand Jews, men, women and children, were gathered into the courtyard of a factory and crammed into cattle cars. Some of the Hungarian townspeople stood watching them go with expressions of satisfaction on their faces. They would inherit the homes and property of the deportees.

A second transport followed, taking away a few of the original townsfolk and the rest of the country Jews, including Cecelia's unmarried brother. With the aunts, uncles and cousins gone, the large house seemed empty and echoing. Aside from her parents, only Cecelia, her divorced sister Esther and her niece Aliza remained. Esther's son, fifteen-year-old Eliezer, was absent. Having no patience for studies, secular or religious, he had run away to Budapest.

The arrangement of a third transport was announced. It was scheduled for a few days later, meant to carry off the last two thousand Jews in town. The Adler family began putting their affairs in order. Cecelia's mother and Esther began distributing clothes and possessions to Gentile neighbors, with a request that they be returned to the first family member who managed to make it back after the war. Yitzchak came to the house to help store the Hebrew books in a chest in the cellar. The family did not want their holy books to be the first victims of the impending disaster. Since childhood, they had kissed these books after every reading, kept them in a place of honor and never used them for any mundane purpose. Respect for sacred literature was second nature to them.

Cecelia happened to be in the room when Yitzchak removed several books from one of the shelves and discovered a bundle of papers that had apparently fallen behind a row of books. He picked them up with an air of puzzlement, then suddenly blanched as he realized what was in the packet.

"What can I do?" he murmured in horror. "Such a valuable thing. Such a valuable thing!"

"What's the matter?" asked his older sister, concerned over his stricken look.

"This is one of the *rebbe's* manuscripts, one of those I never got to work over. This is the only copy in existence, and its safekeeping was my responsibility. I thought it had been returned to Munkacs with all the other volumes."

Through an oversight on his part, one section of the *rebbe's* commentary would now be abandoned to the mercies of thieves and looters, most likely to be used for lighting fires. Cecelia understood now why he looked so appalled. His one desire at this moment was surely to find a way to return this missing object to its owners, but what could he do? Travel by Jews was forbidden, and Yitzchak, with his beard and *peyos*, was conspicuously Jewish. Besides, he could hardly leave his pregnant wife at this time of crisis, just when everyone was to be transported.

With a sudden gesture of decision, Yitzchak set the manuscript down on a table and dispatched his niece Aliza to summon the widow Steinberg. Yitzchak himself disappeared into the kitchen and reappeared shortly, bearing a large tin box now emptied of tea leaves. After turning the box over and tapping the bottom to shake out any stray leaves, he made sure the manuscript would be able to fit in. Assured that it would, he placed the bundle of papers back on the table and set off for the cellar, the tin box held tightly under his arm. Cecelia followed him in curiosity and found him digging a shallow hole in the hard earth floor of the basement, measuring it now and then with the box to determine whether it was sufficiently large. When the hole was wide enough and deep enough to satisfy him, they went back upstairs into the main part of the house and waited for Aliza to return with the widow.

Meanwhile, Yitzchak wrote a note explaining that the materials inside the box were part of a valuable manuscript and requesting the finder to return them to the heirs of the Munkacser Rebbe. He glued the note firmly to the top of the box.

At last, Aliza returned with the widow, whose curiosity was aroused by the peculiar summons. She was a middle-aged woman and had been widowed over twenty-five years. Her husband had been killed fighting in the army of Austro-Hungary during the First World War, leaving her to raise seven children on a small government pension.

With the widow looking on, Yitzchak placed the papers in the box and closed the lid. In a slow and impressive voice, he read the inscription he had pasted on the tin. After swathing the box in a protective layer of cloth, he led them in single file to the basement. Down in the dank cellar, he laid the box in the waiting hole, filled it with earth and tamped it down. The solemnity of his demeanor made the occasion seem like a funeral.

"Note this spot carefully," said Yitzchak to the widow. "Hitler, may his name be blotted out, is beginning to fall. Someday, the Jews will be free to move about again. When that happens, you must come dig this up and send it to Munkacs. It is a valuable and holy work. The responsibility for its survival has fallen on your shoulders. May the *rebbe's* merit protect you in the months to come."

The widow, awed by Yitzchak's solemn voice, nodded dumbly. She glanced around at the walls and ceiling to determine landmarks for the spot, and Cecelia followed suit. She understood, though, why Yitzchak had pinned his hopes on the widow rather than on the members of his own family. It was rumored among the townsfolk that Mrs. Steinberg could expect special treatment from the Germans because she was a war widow from their ally's army.

Yitzchak heaved a sigh, and his tensely held shoulders slumped. He had done everything he could think of to save the book. The three filed upstairs and out into the light. The courtyard looked bright, but in truth, there was only darkness before them, the darkness of an unknown destination.

AUSCHWITZ, POLAND

When the long train ride ended and Cecelia set foot on solid ground again, she was broken in body and in spirit. Six days the journey lasted, six long, torturous days of standing in a cattle car without sanitary facilities, with little food, with insufficient water and almost without air to breathe. She had always been the sickly one in the family, the one her parents worried over. The shock of descending to new, subhuman conditions felt like a plunge into icy water. It was hard for her to believe that she had survived the journey at all. Many others had not.

There were several rows of railroad tracks side by side, and Cecelia might have mistaken the installation for a civilian train station were it not that only prisoners and guards were in sight. On either side of the tracks stood tall, windowless walls. There was no sign indicating location, and Cecelia's mind was too deadened for her to be curious. In the whole miserable situation, she had only one small grain of comfort. She, her sister Esther and her niece Aliza had managed to cling together throughout the journey, and now she trudged alongside them.

On the train platform, the Jews were lined up in single file. Esther was ahead of them with Aliza and Cecelia immediately behind. The line began to move slowly forward, and Cecelia raised her dulled eyes to see what was in store for them now. Up ahead of them was a German officer looking very calm and comfortable in a crisp uniform. The Jews were marched past him one by one. After a brief glance at each, he would point casually either to the left or the right. Thereafter, the line of Jews split into two streams, going off in opposite directions. Cecelia wondered vaguely what the difference was between the two sides, and on what grounds the officer made his choices.

The line moved forward, and soon Esther reached the selection point. After just a flicker of attention, the man waved her to the right. Aliza followed, holding herself as if she had a ramrod in place of a spine, so that she would look older than her thirteen years. A sort of premonition swept through Cecelia, and as Aliza was waved to the right after her mother, Cecelia squared her shoulders and assumed a sprightly expression. The man stared at Cecelia, scrutinizing her from head to toe. Then, almost grudgingly, he waved her to the right after Aliza. Only later that day, when her group was mixed with previous inmates, did she realize the full significance of that gesture. Only then was her attention called to the tall brick smokestacks towering over the camp. Only then did she realize how narrowly she had missed contributing a few grams of her own to the fine ash raining down on the camp.

Her group was assigned to a room lined with three-tiered wooden bunks, six women crowded into each. Cecelia herself was on the top level, and she lay on the hardboards contemplating her surroundings. The air was electric with rumors, rumors about what had happened to the others who had lain on these bunks before them and rumors about where they were destined to go. The camp was said to be in Poland, but almost every woman in the room spoke Hungarian. What had happened to the Polish speakers robust enough to pass the selection? The only trace of them was one young girl acting as a guard, still in the vest she had worn when taken from her home four years before, which by now reached only halfway down her back. What must those four years have been like for her?

Suddenly, a commotion started in one corner of the room and spread in ever-widening ripples along the crowded bunks. Women poured out into the center of the room, jumping and shouting. Only when the message reached Cecelia's bunk did she realize that they were dancing and singing, "We're going home, we're going home!"

Cecelia stared at the happy, raucous crowd. They had all gone insane. Did they really think they had been sent on a six-day journey in a car meant for animals, just to be held for two days and sent home again? Sheer lunacy! Her eyes raked the bunks. As far as she could see, there was not a single other woman in the room who had not been taken in by this rumor.

A swift jolt of fear shot through her. Any crowd, even a crowd of madwomen, was a means of protection, whereas standing out from the crowd could be very dangerous. She frantically began to scramble out of the bunk, but it was too late. She was only down to the second tier of beds when a guard came in to investigate the disturbance.

He stood still for a moment in helpless fury. What could he do to one thousand women suddenly gone wild? Then, almost with relief, he spotted Cecelia, still trying to reach the floor and melt into the mob. In a few strides, he was at her side and began to beat her, raining down insults between the blows.

"You think you are going home alive," he shouted derisively. "No one who passed through here comes out alive!" Blow followed insult, and insult followed blow.

Throughout the torrent of abuse, Cecelia just looked at him, not answering, but only thinking to herself, "If you could see into my soul, you would get down on your knees to beg forgiveness for saying that. Who in this room knows better than I that we will never get home alive?" She gave a fleeting thought to the book her brother had buried and felt a tinge of regret that she would have no part in saving it. It was not to rescue holy books that Heaven had sent her here.

The guard tired of beating her. After one more look at the crowd, he turned and left the room. Let the rest of the women figure out for themselves that they were not going home.

Auschwitz was not their last stop. Instead, they were loaded back into the cattle cars and carried off to a forced-labor camp. They were temporarily lodged in a commandeered chateau, but soon they were marched on foot to an installation built to hold prisoners, with barracks each holding seventy-five women. The wired fences around the camp were not as sophisticated as the electrified fences at Auschwitz, and a few women tried to escape. The attempts were doomed to failure. Could one escape when all the countryside was in sympathy with their captors? Those who made the effort to get away were caught and shot immediately.

Cecelia, like the other women in her barracks, worked in an armaments factory. Whenever she noticed a flaw in one of the parts she was laboring over, she cringed. They were punished for every defective part they allowed past, and they were punished equally hard for any acceptable part they discarded. Cecelia puzzled over the one in front of her at the moment. Did that small crack justify throwing out the whole piece?

She carried the item over to the SS man supervising them and held it out on the palm of her hand.

"Excuse me, sir," she asked. "Is this part too flawed to use?"

Astounded at her impertinence, he delivered an open-handed slap which knocked her backwards and sent the part flying. She stumbled, falling out of his reach.

"Back to work, filthy Jew," he snarled. "Keep your pesky questions to yourself."

Cecelia retrieved the now broken piece and crept back to her station. Under a submissive mien, she seethed at the injustice. They were held responsible for the quality of the parts, without being allowed to know how they were to be judged. At least she was wiser now about one thing. She would never ask another question at this job.

In order to remain alive, it would not suffice for her heart to continue beating and for her lungs to continue drawing in air. She also had to look productive. The prisoners were periodically inspected, and any woman whose strength seemed exhausted was removed from the group and sent to one of the extermination camps. That small, weak Cecelia squeaked through one such examination after another was a sign both of an iron determination to live and of special protection from Heaven.

Hunger, weariness and fear did not exhaust the discomforts of their lives. They were cold and underdressed, as well. When they had first passed through the selection point at Auschwitz, they had been stripped of all clothing and possessions except for their shoes, and all their hair had been shaved off. The shoes Cecelia had been wearing had been a good, stout pair. After a month or so in the camp, her feet and legs began to swell, a symptom of the starvation diet. Keeping the shoes fastened became something of a problem, but she was still grateful for the warmth and protection from dampness they afforded. This comfort, however, did not continue indefinitely. On one of the rare occasions when the women were assigned outdoor labor, she happened to stand on hot coals without noticing what she was doing. Her shoes protected her feet this one last time, but they themselves were completely ruined. As a replacement, she was issued a clumsy pair of wooden shoes which kept her feet neither warm nor dry.

In Auschwitz, Cecelia had inherited, from some unfortunate woman who had been sent to the gas chambers, a piece of clothing so scanty that it could scarcely be called a dress. It was a source of great shame to her to be walking about half-clothed, and she determined to find a way to acquire material for a decent garment. One day, she performed one of the bravest acts possible for prisoners under their conditions. She voluntarily gave up her daily bread ration. With that bread, a currency more valuable than gold, she bought from another prisoner a piece of cloth from which she sewed a dress. After she put it on, she began to feel like a human being again.

When they were first brought from Auschwitz to their temporary quarters in the old chateau, Cecelia got something of a shock. She caught a reflection of the room she was standing in, mirrored in a darkened window. There, reflected among the faces of the other women in the room, was the face of a man. She spun around to see where he was standing, but there was no such person in view. Nonplussed, she turned back to the window. The strange face was still there.

"Esther," she called to her sister. "Come and look! There's a man's face here but no man in the room."

Esther came over, glanced in the direction Cecelia was pointing and smiled faintly.

"It's a sad state we've come to," she sighed, "when you cannot even recognize your own face."

Cecelia's eyes widened, and so did the eyes of the image in the glass. She moved over close to the window and peered intently at the faint reflection of a figure with close-cropped hair, gaunt cheeks, sunken eyes, more like a skeleton than a human being. Indeed, it was a sad state they had come to.

Some of the workers in the armaments factory were not Jewish prisoners. One of these was a local woman who had been sentenced to two days a week of forced labor as punishment for perpetrating some offense against the National Socialist regime. Since she was not there every day, she was moved around from place to place in the production line, and one day she happened to be placed next to Cecelia. Toward the end of the day, Cecelia felt something being thrust into her clothing. It was a very disconcerting feeling, and she jerked conspicuously. The other prisoners around, who had had previous experience with this particular German woman, gave each other knowing smiles. Fearing the guards, Cecelia made no effort to investigate the strange lump inside her dress front until the shift was over. As soon as she reached a spot where she was unobserved, she discovered that the woman had given her, as a present, two whole apples.

There was no question of keeping them all for herself. She would surely share them with Esther and her niece Aliza. As she thought of Aliza, a wave of pity swept over her. Her niece was still growing, and her young body desperately craved food. She was unable, like her elders, to stretch out her bread ration over a period of hours by eating it crumb by crumb. Instead, she swallowed it up in an instant and looked around for more. How much she must need the vitamins in this fruit! Cecelia decided to give both apples, in their entirety, to her niece.

She found Aliza, who was on her way to visit a sick friend. The young girl thanked her gratefully and concealed the fruit in her clothing. Only when she returned did her aunt discover that, in a parallel gesture of generosity, she had given both apples to the patient. Her aunt was furious. Did not the foolish child realize that her sick friend worked outside and had access to other food? Those precious vitamins were wasted on her.

One day, poking around in a trash heap, Cecelia found a real treasure, a whole sprouting onion. She took it into the washroom and poured stream after stream of water over it, until not the slightest trace remained of its sojourn in the garbage. She, Esther and Aliza had a feast from that onion.

The approach of winter aggravated the food shortage. The cold not only brought increased discomfort, but also the need for an increased number of calories for simply maintaining body temperature. At the same time, the food deliveries to the camp grew smaller, presumably because of the military situation and the inadequacy of winter stockpiles. The soups were thinner, and the guards more irritable.

Once, while coming out of the barracks, Cecelia noticed someone slip furtively past her with a potato in each of her hands.

"Quick," she whispered to Esther. "Someone found potatoes somewhere over there."

Esther grabbed something to use as a bag and raced off, with Cecelia hobbling along behind as fast as she could go. Other women passed her carrying potatoes, and she realized that a whole bag must have broken somewhere. When Cecelia caught up to her sister, she found that all the potatoes were already gone, except for a few Esther had gathered into her bag, and one last one that she was reaching for. At that moment, one of the guards arrived, barking, "What's going on here?"

Esther straightened out to face him, the last potato still held in her hand. The guard was almost shaking with rage as he realized that this lowly prisoner had almost succeeded in stealing some food. Cecelia was tense with fright. What would they do to Esther? Would she be whipped? Tortured? Shot? Esther showed no signs at all of fear. She held herself like a queen and glared at the guard as if he were a dog.

"Haul her out!" screamed the guard to his helpers. "Cut off all her hair!"

Cecelia let out her breath in a burst. Was that all? It was too good to believe. As it turned out, that was not quite all. They also made Esther clean the latrines for a week. Compared to what might have been, though, it was nothing. Food thefts were high crime in the camp.

Spring came, the spring of 1945. One day, a very peculiar group of Germans appeared in the camp. They began to go about among the prisoners and speak to them. When some German came over to Cecelia and asked her how she was feeling, she just looked at him as if he had gone mad, and she did not utter a word. As strangely as they had come, the group disappeared again.

That day the rations were unusually skimpy. In the evening, thirty women sat around in the darkened hut, unable to speak of anything except their hunger. Cecelia sat in a corner, fingering a lump in her pocket. Carefully, so that no one else would notice, she pulled it out and sat with her hands cupped around the small object. It was a parsnip.

For weeks, she had been saving it. She had found it in the garbage and rinsed it absolutely clean. Resisting the ever-present temptation to pounce on any scrap of food and consume it immediately, she had decided that this parsnip should be saved for a day when she was about to die of starvation. Then she would have something to comfort her.

What should she do now? It was true that she was fainting with starvation, but how could she eat when everyone else was equally hungry? On the other hand, if she shared it among all thirty of them, each woman would get a piece so small it would not help at all. No, there was no point in trying to share it, but she would not eat alone when all her friends were starving. She slipped the parsnip discreetly back into her pocket. Eventually, despite the hunger pangs, everyone went to sleep.

In the early morning, the block warden, the senior prisoner in charge of organizing them, came in and woke them all up.

"I have an announcement to make," she said. "I want you all to promise that you will listen quietly. I want no shouting or hysterics."

The prisoners looked at each other in puzzlement. Shouting? Hysterics? They were so weak they could barely sit up in bed. They readily promised to be perfectly calm.

"Good," said the block warden. "This is my announcement: You are free."

There was a brief moment of stunned silence, and then an uproar of shrieking and crying. Women who, a moment before, could barely lift an arm, were jumping up and down embracing each other. There was a mad scramble for the kitchens, but in vain. All the guards had run away during the night, taking with them everything edible. Not even a stick of margarine remained in the empty larder.

Cecelia, Esther and Aliza walked out through the open front gate to the neighboring village and begged a few pieces of bread from the townspeople. Only then did Cecelia notice that she still had the parsnip tucked away in her pocket. How its importance had fallen!

The winds that swept through Europe that year, driving refugees hither and thither, deposited Cecelia and her family in Pressburg, Hungary. Three women alone, they lacked the strength to push themselves aboard one of the overloaded trains heading toward Budapest and home, so they remained where they were, eating at a kosher soup kitchen which had been set up by one of the relief organizations for Jewish refugees.

Standing in line in the public kitchen one day, Cecelia noticed a Russian soldier stalk in through the door in the back. Since the Red Army troops were notorious throughout Eastern

Europe for their brutality against those they conquered, she was instantly on guard. Bareheaded, hair cut short and one arm in a sling, he obviously had no place in a Jewish soup kitchen. He scanned the crowd, his eyes rested on them, and he started to advance. Esther was looking in a different direction, and before Cecelia could warn her of the danger, the soldier was already at Esther's side. Esther swung around in surprise.

"Mama?" the man asked.

"I'm afraid you must have made some mistake," said Esther, flustered.

"Mama, don't you recognize me? It's me. Eli."

A very different Eli it was from the one who had left home two years earlier at age fifteen. Gone were the *tzitzis* and the cap. He had grown several inches, his shoulders had filled out, and there was stubble on his cheeks. He had served in a band of partisans in Budapest until the Russians had conquered the city. Then he had joined the Russian army in their advance across Hungary and Austria. He had stayed with the army as far as Vienna, where he had been wounded. Released from service, he had begun making inquiries among the swelling throngs of Jewish refugees for word of his mother and sister and had heard a rumor that they had been seen in Pressburg. The obvious place to search first had been in the soup kitchen, and he had been rewarded immediately.

With Eli to shoulder a path for them through the crowds, the four were soon on a train headed back to Budapest. Eli hoped some of his partisan contacts might be able to find them quarters in the city.

It was extremely crowded in the train, but it was such an improvement over the cattle cars that Cecelia barely minded. Who knows? With this auspicious beginning, they might soon be reunited with yet more members of their family.

As soon as they got off the train in Budapest, they met

someone from their home city of Beregszasz.

"Have you seen anyone from our family?" asked Esther eagerly.

The girl shook her head sadly.

"No one you should expect to see," she replied. "I was with your sister Fruma and her children, but they will never come home."

"You mean . . . ?"

The girl nodded gently.

With a wail, Cecelia and Esther sank down to the floor and wept. This was the first definite word they had heard about the fate of members of their family. A full year of worrying and wondering poured out in those sobs. Then, when the first installment of tears was paid, Cecelia put her hand on Esther's shoulder.

"Come," Cecelia said. "We cannot cry here all night. We must go and look for shelter."

They found it in a school designated as a temporary haven for refugees returning from the camps. They registered with the kosher kitchen to obtain meals. It took them two days to get somewhat settled, and then Cecelia made her announcement to Esther.

"I'm going home," she said. "Don't tell anyone. You can draw my ration and share it with the children till I return."

Esther balked at the plan. For a year now, they had clung together, and now Cecelia wanted to set off alone through an anti-Semitic country.

"Remember how pleased all the Hungarians were to see us all carried away, our property left behind?" Esther warned.

"That's why I'm not going back to stay," agreed Cecelia. "But I have to make one short visit. I need to fetch something, a book of Yitzchak's, and I want to see if anyone else has gotten back."

Esther raised other objections, but Cecelia would listen to none of them. Early the next morning, she climbed onto the train.

BEREGSZASZ, HUNGARY

C ecelia was huddled in an abandoned dwelling, shaken by sobs. In her moments of greatest despair, she beat her head against the wall in the hope she would die. She could find no reason for living. For the first time, from the few Jews who had straggled back to Beregszasz, she had heard the full story of what had been done to the Jews of Europe. Her parents, her brothers, her sisters, her uncles, her aunts, her cousins, all had been gassed and burned to cinders.

Day after day, the sobs continued to shake her weak, starved body. She fell sick and grew delirious. She refused to eat and gave over her rations to a mother with children. In her wilder moments, she actually tried to break her head against the wall, but even during saner periods she did not intend to recover from this illness.

One morning, as she lay limply on her pallet, she overheard two women discussing her serious condition. One suggested buying medicine, and the other pointed out that they had no money.

"We could take up a collection for her," suggested the first woman.

Cecelia was so horrified that she almost sat up. To this she had sunk! People were going to collect charity for her! If only her mother had been laid in a grave, she would have turned over at the thought. Cecelia realized she would have to pull herself together.

She began to eat again. Bit by bit, a little strength began to return, and she started to lay plans for the day when she could be up and about. She still had to find Yitzchak's book, and then she would rejoin her sister and the children in Budapest. Together, they would all emigrate to someplace where she would not feel herself surrounded by people who would prefer to see her dead. Any day now, she would be ready for the trip to her family's house to dig up the book.

The final piece of bad news reached Cecelia while she was still recuperating. The Russians drew a new, closed border between Russia and Hungary, with Beregszasz and Munkacs on the Russian side.

Cecelia in Beregszasz, Russia, was cut off from her sister in Budapest, Hungary!

Cecelia stood outside the dusty window of what had once been her family's dining room. Neighbors used to stand at this window late on *Pesach* night, to hear her family sing the songs at the end of the *Seder*. Now the only sounds to be heard through it were the moos and neighs of the animals stabled there by its current owner.

Picking her way through the filth in the courtyard she used to keep so well-tended, she headed for the steps to the cellar. A young man, a friend of her brother Yitzchak, followed closely behind. She was nearly at the head of the steps when she heard a window open in the next house.

"What are you doing fooling around in my stable?" yelled a man leaning out the window.

"This was our house!" she shouted back defiantly.

The man decided not to press the matter and slammed the window shut again.

The young man descended the cellar steps first, and Cecelia followed. Not until she was out of sight of the yard did she light the candle she had brought. All the furniture they had stored there, and every other object of value, had been taken by looters.

What else could she have expected? Even neighbors to whom they had given clothes for safekeeping had refused to return them.

Cecelia found the spot where her brother had buried the tin container. It was not hard to remember the day he had buried it. It was engraved deeply in her memory. How pained her brother had been at the thought that the manuscript might be lost because he had overlooked it! Now the responsibility to return it had fallen on her own hunched shoulders.

Cecelia and the *yeshivah* boy began scratching the earthen floor with scraps of wood they found lying nearby. There were no signs of previous digging in the floor, so it would seem that the looters had not suspected the cellar of harboring buried treasures. The box should be just where her brother had buried it, not very far below the surface.

Since so many things in Cecelia's life had not worked out the way they should have, she was surprised when her stick met the resistance she had been expecting. The two scraped away the dirt covering the tin lid and widened the hole until all four edges were clear. Slowly, they eased the tin container out of the hole. The cloth in which the box had been wrapped was completely rotten, but the label on which her brother had explained the contents of the container was as white and crisp as on the day he had written it. Cecelia loosened the lid and took a peek inside. Indeed, the manuscript was still there. Closing it again tightly, she climbed to her feet, clutching the box. She was not planning to let it out of her possession until she personally could deliver it to Munkacs.

They pushed the dirt back into the hole and stomped it down lightly to avoid arousing unwelcome accusations by the current master of the house. They turned and left the cellar together. It was fortunate that her brother's friend had recognized her in the street and had introduced himself; she had been afraid to make this expedition by herself. Not that it had been an accident, of course; there are no accidents in this world. This manuscript had been destined to come to light, and Providence had kept her alive because she was in the position to save it; why else had she been brought back to this place where nothing else remained for her? The book had made a liar of the guard in Auschwitz who had beaten her so fiercely. She *had* returned home alive.

It took over a week to make arrangements for the trip to Munkacs, a week of hovering around the box like a mother bird guarding her eggs. In time, she got together the money for a round-trip ticket and arrived by bus in the Munkacs station. Once, *chassidim* by the hundreds, her brother among them, had gotten off at this station to visit the *rebbe*. Now she did not know if any Jews were left in town at all. Holding tightly onto the bag containing the book, she set off in search of the remnant of the *chassidic* court.

A pitiful remnant it was, when she found it. A few *chassidim* had straggled back, but the *rebbe* and his close disciples were all gone. She explained her mission, but no one seemed willing to take responsibility for the manuscript. The *rebbe's* heir was in America, and they felt that if the book were mailed it would probably be confiscated by the Russian authorities. There was no possibility of having it published under a Stalinist regime.

Cecelia was stunned. For weeks now, she had been obsessed with this mission. She had gathered all her energy for this one long trip to unburden herself of the responsibility, and she had been rebuffed.

Weary and heartsick, she trudged out to the Jewish cemetery, threw herself down on the grave of the *rebbe* who had written the commentary and began to weep. She wept not only for herself, but for her brother, her parents, her family, her entire lost world. There was no one left to whom she could turn for advice, no one who could tell her what to do.

Cecelia wept until she was emptied of tears. A tiny, frail figure, bones almost bare of flesh, she lay on the grave wishing she, too, were dead with the rest of them. With a sigh, she sat up and stared blankly at the book. Because she had returned for this book she was now cut off from building a new life in another country. Should she leave the book here on the grave of the holy one who had written it? That might be a fitting end to its journey, but the thought of the rain beating down on it and washing the ink off the pages was more than she could bear after all the trouble she had taken to preserve it. As so often in the last year, she reminded herself that if she was frail in body, then she must become strong in spirit. She would force those at Munkacs to take the book. Perhaps someone would read it someday, and all her suffering would not have been in vain.

Trudging back to town, she again sought out the Munkacs synagogue and demanded to speak to the most important man there. One of those sitting at the table shook his head mournfully.

"Sad. Sad. It is a dreary day for Munkacs when I must say I am the leader here."

Cecelia laid the book on the table and told the entire story of its rescue.

"It belongs here," she concluded. "I pass on the trust to you."

The man, a ritual slaughterer of animals by trade, shrugged.

"There are no scholars left in Munkacs to study it," he said. "It will lie on the shelf unused."

"What would it do on my shelf?" countered Cecelia. "My brother told me to return it to the court in Munkacs, and that is what I have done."

She took her leave and walked out of the synagogue. The orphaned book remained behind in its new foster home, while Cecelia returned to the city in which she had once lived so happily, but which had now turned into a prison.

BEREGOVO, U.S.S.R.

C ecelia Adler continued to live in her hometown after her return from the concentration camps. With the border to the West sealed, there was nowhere else for her to go. The attitude of the Russian officials toward the survivors added a new insult to the list of all her sufferings.

"If you returned alive," they told her, "you must have collaborated with the Germans."

This filled her completely with bitterness; to be told that she had collaborated with the murderers of her parents and siblings!

Her first need was for some way to earn a living. Her self-respect was still intact, and it was unthinkable that an Adler should accept any charity. She was unwilling to become involved in anything dishonest; that value had been instilled in her by her upbringing. Neither could she have looked for work in a factory, for that would have required working on *Shabbos*, which she refused to do.

Most of the families who straggled back from the camps were no longer religiously observant. She found a few congenial souls among the families of the professionals—a doctor, an apothecary, a lawyer, people who had known and respected her parents before the war. They provided her some comfort, a slight echo of the warmth and comfort of the past, but in all matters of the spirit she was totally isolated.

She had never been particularly religious. She had, of course, kept all the rituals and laws, whatever was necessary, and had tried to do what was right, but all that had been very natural. Unlike her brother Yitzchak, she had never been given to deep thought on religious matters, nor did she have much formal education in Hebrew. She could pronounce the words in the prayer book, but that was all. All she had were memories of how things had been done in her parents' home.

Her captors had broken her body in the camps, but they had forced her to strengthen her soul until it was unbreakable. She would continue to do whatever was necessary, no matter how difficult. In the camps, under the threat of immediate starvation or execution, she had eaten non-kosher food and worked on *Shabbos*, but now she was free. Even if she were the only person in town to do so, she was resolved to observe the laws of the Torah as she had in her parents' house. But how was a frail, forty-year-old woman in communist Russia to find honest employment that did not involve desecrating *Shabbos*?

A friend, the apothecary, found a solution. He granted her a franchise to sell non-prescription remedies in a small stand in the street and told her which medicines to offer for which complaints. If someone came with a headache, she sold him the white tablets. If he had a cough, there was brown syrup to be given. Cecelia herself spoke only Hungarian and the little German she had learned in school, but she learned the words for "headache," "stomach-ache" and so forth in Russian, well enough to dispense her small store of remedies to all comers. However, though she sat in the cold in her open stall every day besides *Shabbos*, the percentage she received from the sales barely sufficed to buy bread, and she could not afford coal to heat the small room she rented.

Jewish holidays that fell on a weekday gave her special cause for fear. She was afraid she might be reported to the police by some disappointed customer. She would put on her white apothecary's smock and sit trembling in the stall with the window closed, so that if the police arrived she would be on the spot and could claim that she closed the stall for only a short time to take a break. How different was a *Rosh Hashanah* spent locked in the cold stall, from the joyous festivals she had always known in her parents' home!

The doctor's family and her other friends saw how pinched

she was for money, and they tried in every way they could think of to get her to accept some supplement from them—if not money, then at least a present. Clothing was very scarce in those first years after the war, and there were known cases of men who had murdered just to steal the victim's shoes. Cecelia continued to wear the one dress she had brought out of the concentration camp for several years, and it pained her friends to see the daughter of a once wealthy family still wearing tattered clothes. Cecelia, however, was adamant in refusing all gifts.

One day, the druggist's wife decided that she would have to be more forceful. She came with her daughter to pay a visit to Cecelia, and the two women chatted amicably. After half an hour, she stood up, preparing to leave. She pulled a package wrapped in brown paper from her satchel.

"I'm leaving this here with you," she said abruptly, and she and her daughter fled from the room before Cecelia could say another word.

Cecelia, slightly numbed by the suddenness of their exit, turned the bundle over. The paper opened, revealing two lengths of material. How dare they! Cecelia rewrapped the package to protect it from prying eyes, tucked it under her arm and set out for the druggist's home. She rapped on the door but there was no answer. Her second knock also produced no response, but it seemed to her that one of the curtains in the window near the porch had swayed slightly. Convinced that her friend was at home, but hiding, Cecelia gave a third knock, deposited the bundle on the door sill and marched back to her own room.

The battle was not yet over. One *Purim*, when Cecelia was struggling to finish her cooking and baking in time for the holiday meal, the druggist's wife and daughter paid another visit. Cecelia forced herself to be polite and sociable, though actually she was anxious to return to her unfinished work in the kitchen. There was a knock on the door, and Cecelia opened it to find a postman standing in the hall. He stepped forward to lay a package on the table. He then threw up his hands and raced out of the room as if he had just noticed the ceiling starting to collapse, before Cecelia had a chance to say a word.

Cecelia turned the package over, but there was no return address anywhere on the paper. She took off her apron, excused herself to her guest and walked out with the bundle, without even opening it to see what was inside. She went to the ritual slaughterer, who was the highest ranking religious functionary in town.

"I want it to be announced in the synagogue," she requested, "that this was lost at my home. Whoever can tell you what is inside can claim it."

The man took the package, and only then did Cecelia feel free to return to her kitchen.

In the battle to avoid taking charity, Cecelia had emerged victorious. Her friends desisted from further attempts for fear of offending her. To her mind, however, it was a negative sort of victory. Her parents had not only avoided taking; they had also given with open hands. Cecelia, too, had spent her early life aiding others. Never having been well enough to marry, she had remained at home caring for the house while her mother tended the family store. It was Cecelia who had swept out the house every day, tended the garden and cared for her divorced sister's two children. What now did she have to give? She was of no use to anyone at all.

The idea came to her one winter as she noticed the envious glances her friends gave the Christmas trees in their neighbors' homes. Poor things, they did not even know that the Jews had special holidays of their own. Nothing was observed in their homes, and those families who did still keep the festivals did so behind locked doors, hidden from the prying eyes of the secret police and hidden also from the eyes of the Jewish children.

Here was something Cecelia could do—she could show these children there was a brighter side to being Jewish, that it was not entirely a matter of persecutions and atrocities. She thought back to her own childhood. She and her siblings had rejoiced on each festival just because it was a festival. It is true that there were special treats and excellent meals, but that was an incidental ingredient of the holiday atmosphere. These poor children, growing up, knew nothing. How could they rejoice that righteous Esther defeated wicked Haman, if they had never heard of either? She would have to attract them with glitter and sweets.

From the moment Cecelia conceived her plan, her life was transformed. Although there are only a few holidays in a year, the preparations began to give a new meaning to every day of her life. Colored paper was hard to obtain, so whenever she noticed a piece drifting along the street, she would pounce on it and tuck it away for making *sukkah* decorations. Whenever she found a strong, straight stick in a bundle of firewood, she would put it aside for making *Simchas Torah* flags. In the evenings, after returning from work, she would prepare those things which could be made in advance. She whittled *Chanukah* tops out of wood and carved into the sides the letters standing for "a great miracle happened there." All year long, whenever a freshly minted coin would pass through her hands, she would put it aside for "*Chanukah* money" for the children. She saved candle stubs all year long for use in lighting up the *Simchas Torah* procession.

The pace of the preparations accelerated as each holiday approached. The first party she made for the children was on *Purim*. She baked large gingerbread cookies and frosted them with the faces of Mordechai, Queen Esther and King Achashveirosh. She spent almost two hours decorating the *challah*, making it attractive with raisins and other delicacies.

When her friends' children came in and saw the table she had spread for them, their eyes widened and they stood fixed in their places at the door. Cecelia had to lead them forward and explain the meaning of each thing before them. She told them of wicked Haman's plot to destroy the Jews in the Persian Empire and of their miraculous escape. They admired every detail on the royal cookies, from the golden crowns to the rouge on Esther's cheek, and then nibbled their way through the heroes of the *Purim* story. The occasion was a tremendous success, and Cecelia would have no trouble obtaining guests for her next party.

Teaching the children about *Sukkos* presented something of a problem. Although it was legal for Cecelia to practice her religion in the privacy of her own apartment, it was a punishable crime to teach it to someone else's children. She could not possibly make a *sukkah* out of doors, but it pained her not to teach them anything about a custom so likely to capture their imagination. Finally, she decided on a compromise. She removed all the clothing from the wardrobe standing in one corner of her room, and decorated the inside walls as one would decorate a *sukkah*, fastening branches to the ceiling of the wardrobe to simulate the branches with which a real *sukkah* would be roofed. The palm frond and citron waved during the festival were unobtainable, but she made models to simulate them. The walls were hung with sheets, and to these she pinned all the little chains, stars and other trinkets she had fashioned out of her collection of strayed paper.

In honor of *Simchas Torah*, Cecelia would sacrifice ten precious potatoes. She cut them in half and hollowed out sockets to hold the candle stubs she had saved. The children who caught sight of her in the street on the way to the synagogue would flock around clamoring for a flag, but she could not permit them to be displayed on the street. Only when they were inside the building and the dancing had started would she unwrap her package of banners, attach a potato and candle to the top of each stick and distribute the prizes to her young friends.

For the months before *Chanukah,* Cecelia would hoard away some of the money she usually spent on food, until she finally had enough saved to buy an entire kilo of sugar cubes. After the children had eaten the cakes she had prepared for them and been told about the wicked Antiochus, they all sat on the floor to play with the tops she had whittled, in the light of the *Chanukah* candles. Whenever the top would land with its highest letter up, Cecelia would reward the spinner with a cube of sugar. She herself would spin for those too small to spin the tops and saw to it that every child was a winner. As the top would begin to wobble and finally flip over, the children could not contain their shrieks of elation or disappointment at the result.

Unknown to Cecelia, one of her neighbors in the multi-story apartment building became curious about the periodic visits of so many noisy children to her otherwise quiet neighbor's apartment. One day, she stopped one or two small stragglers and began to question them.

"You've been having a nice time, haven't you? What have you all been doing there in Miss Adler's house?"

"She made us a party," confided the beaming child.

"A party? How lovely. Was there any special reason for a celebration?"

"It was a *Chanukah* party," explained the child, proud of his newfound knowledge. "Today is *Chanukah.*"

Cecelia was summoned by the state police. The initials and the upper ranks of this organization were changed from time to time, but it was always intimidating. After a tense wait, Cecelia was called into a room where two men began to interrogate her. They asked questions about a wide range of subjects. Where did she live? What had she done during the war? How was she employed? Who were her friends. Cecelia was unable, from the

range of questions, to discover what exactly it was they suspected her of.

They had called her in once before, but that time it was only
as an auxiliary witness. When the family had been deported by
the Germans, a Hungarian dentist had offered to hide one of her
nieces, the daughter of one of her married sisters. Her grateful
mother had given him a large sum of money for her support. A
few days later, the girl had been delivered to the concentration
camp where her mother was imprisoned. Keeping all the money
for himself, the dentist had turned her over to the Germans. The
interrogation about that had been more straightforward, but
Cecelia had not been able to give any useful testimony, since she
had already been on her way to Auschwitz at the time. The man
was never convicted, and he continued to practice peacefully in
town, numbering some Jewish children among his patients.
Whenever Cecelia saw him coming she crossed to the other side
of the street as quickly as possible.

If that interrogation had been straightforward, this one was
just the opposite, and Cecelia could not tell which subjects she
should be most guarded about. Did they know that she closed
her stall on *Shabbos* and *Yom Tov*? Had they found out about the
parties for the children? Were they renewing the accusation that
she was a collaborator? The questions streamed on.

"What was your father's name?" they demanded.

"Amshel Asher," she answered.

"What was your mother's name?"

"Chanah."

The two men straightened and looked at each other. "Chanah
. . . Chanah . . . Chanah-ka!"

A few minutes later, Cecelia found herself free and on her
way home. Now it was clear why she had been detained. Some
neighbor had found out about the *Chanukah* party and informed
on her, without knowing what *Chanukah* was. G-d, in his

mercy, had put into the minds of her interrogators the idea that she had invited the children to celebrate her mother's name-day. Feeling a little embarrassed over their supposed mistake, they let her go without further investigation.

Cecelia continued her parties for the children for all the twenty-five years she remained in Beregszasz, or Beregovo, as the Russians renamed it. The police themselves had taught her what cover story to use. She always trained the children that if anyone should ask them what they were doing at her house, they should say they were celebrating her mother's name-day. The parties *were*, in a sense, a memorial to her parents. Only two of her many siblings survived the war. She herself had no progeny at all. By bringing a little of the heritage she had received to the children of Beregszasz, she was doing her best to pass it on.

The manuscript Cecelia was entrusted with had been smuggled out from behind the Iron Curtain while Cecelia was still in Russia, but it was not actually published until she was granted an exit visa and joined her sister in Israel in 1970. A lawyer came to interview her about her brother and the history of the manuscript. The story is printed in the introduction to the book. She received five complimentary copies of the volume, but being both poor and warm-hearted, she gave them all away as *bar-mitzvah* presents. She felt her true reward was knowing that, in the end, her brother's wish had been fulfilled.